TANKER OPERATIONS
A Handbook for the Ship's Officer

A multi-point offshore mooring. Oil cargoes are transferred between ship and shore via submarine pipelines. The Ralph M. Parsons Company.

TANKER
OPERATIONS

A Handbook for the Ship's Officer

G.S. Marton

CORNELL MARITIME PRESS, INC.

CAMBRIDGE   1978   MARYLAND

Library of Congress Cataloging in Publication Data

Marton, Greg S   1948-
    Tanker operations.

    Bibliography: p.
    Includes index.
    1. Tankers--Handbooks, manuals, etc.   I. Title.
VM455.M33   623.88'2'45   77-17148
ISBN 0—87033—240-6

CONTENTS

In memory of Philip C. Marton

PREFACE

A number of years ago, when I was beginning my career on oil tankers, I often felt the lack of a simple, straightforward handbook on the basic problems of tanker operations. Hence, this book. *Tanker Operations: A Handbook for the Ship's Officer* is directed primarily toward the newcomer to tankers; specifically, the new officer. Generally speaking, it is not a step-by-step manual covering every possible situation. Instead, it is intended as:

1. An introductory guide designed to make the new officer's adjustment to tanker life smoother, less perilous.

2. A source of useful information for the more experienced officer.

3. A reference book for other individuals interested in the operation of oil tankers, particularly those aspiring to the rating of tankerman.

I should point out, however, that tankers cannot be learned entirely from a book. The tankerman's job is too complex and, in many ways, intuitive. Moreover, each tanker is unique and must be learned individually.

Fortunately, the learning process is not an entirely lonely task. Shipmates—pumpmen, fellow officers, sailors—all have knowledge to share, and some make excellent teachers. In the end, however, the way to learn a tanker is to put on a boiler suit and, flashlight in hand, explore every corner of the vessel, learning pumproom, piping systems, valves. This is a tedious, sometimes exhausting process, but it must be done. An officer unwilling to make this effort should forget about a career, even a brief one, on tankers.

Some tankers, old and rusty, are relics of a bygone era. Others are so futuristic, so thoroughly automated, that their crew members feel more like astronauts than tankermen. And, in all likelihood, the future tankerman will need the training and temperament of an astronaut.

Regardless of age or equipment, however, all tankers perform the same basic task—they carry oil. Their voyages span the globe, from the blazing deserts of Saudi Arabia to the frozen shores of the Arctic. Through it all, tankermen are accompanied by the pungent smells of crude oil and gasoline, by loneliness, tension, exhaustion . . . and the satisfaction of doing a job well. No individual can adequately describe this unique way of life. It must be experienced firsthand.

I would like to take this opportunity to thank the many individuals and organizations who were kind enough to help me in this effort. Some showed remarkable patience with my repeated requests for information, research materials, and illustrations.

Special thanks to:

The American Bureau of Shipping; American Cast Iron Pipe Company; American Institute of Marine Underwriters; American Institute of Merchant Shipping; American Petroleum Institute; the Ansul Company; Apex Marine Corporation; Atlantic Richfield Company; the Scott Aviation Division of ATO, Inc.; Mrs. Gerry Bayless; Bethlehem Steel Corporation; Bingham-Willamette Company; British Petroleum Company, Ltd.; Henry Browne & Son, Ltd.; Butterworth Systems, Inc.; Chevron Shipping Company; Coppus Engineering Corporation; Exxon Corporation and Exxon Company (U.S.A.); FMC Corporation; Mr. Steve Faulkner; Mr. Bill Finhandler; Gamlen Chemical Company; General Dynamics Corporation; General Fire Extinguisher Corporation; Mr. R.W. Gorman; Gulf Oil Corporation; Mr. Arthur Handt; Hendy International Company; the Penco Division of the Hudson Engineering Company; Mr. John Hunter; Huntington Alloys, Inc.; the Keystone Valve Division of Keystone International, Inc.; Kockums Automation AB; Mr. Gene D. Legler; the Harry Lundeberg School; Mine Safety Appliances Company; Mr. C. Bradford Mitchell; National Audubon Society; National Foam System, Inc.; National Maritime Union of America; National Steel and Shipbuilding Company; Miss Maureen Ott; the Ralph M. Parsons Company; Paul-Munroe Hydraulics, Inc.; Mrs. Pia Philipp; Phillips Petroleum Company; Sailors' Union of the Pacific; Salen & Wicander AB; San Francisco Maritime Museum; E.W. Saybolt & Company, Inc.; Mr. W.F. Schill; Seafarers International Union; Shell International Petroleum and Shell Oil Company (U.S.A.); Shipbuilders Council of America; Sperry Marine Systems; Sun Shipbuilding and Dry Dock Company; Mr. Bob Sutherland; Underwriters Laboratories, Inc.; United States Coast Guard; United States Maritime Administration; U.S. Salvage Association; Valve Manufacturers Association; West Coast Ship Chandlers, Inc.; Worthington Pump Corporation.

G.S.M.

TANKER OPERATIONS
A Handbook for the Ship's Officer

Chapter 1

WHAT IS AN OIL TANKER?

The first oil tanker was launched less than a hundred years ago. In this relatively short time, tankers have evolved into efficient, oil-moving machines—the largest mobile objects ever constructed.

Every tanker, whether a small coastwise vessel or a mammoth super-ship, is basically a hollow steel shell subdivided into tanks by longitudinal and transverse bulkheads (Fig. 1). The engine room is located aft, as is the bridge on newer ships.

A system of pipelines fitted along the bottom of the tank range carries oil to and from the tanks. Pumps are used for discharging; these are installed in one or more pumprooms which in turn are connected to a main-deck manifold by additional piping. Oil is transferred from ship to shore and vice versa by means of flexible hoses and steel loading arms which bolt onto the ship's manifold.

Tankers come in all sizes and designs. They carry a variety of products, consisting mainly of crude oil and its derivatives: gasoline, diesel fuel, stove oil, bunker fuel, kerosene, jet fuel, and many others. In addition, a few specialized vessels carry exotic cargoes such as wine, vegetable oil, and molasses.

The type of cargo a tanker carries largely determines the complexity of her operation and, consequently, the amount of sweat and concentration required from her officers.

LEARNING THE HARD WAY

I learned the significance of the foregoing statement early in my career. My first third mate's job was on a 17,000-ton coastwise tanker. She was in black-oil service, mainly hauling crude and heavy fuel oil. As a rule, she carried one commodity at a time, sometimes two. The operation was simple and I caught on quickly.

But I was in for a shock; after a month on the black-oil ship, I was transferred to another vessel—a so-called "drug store" carrying refined products.

She hauled a hodgepodge of cargoes—a dozen or more at a time—all of which were kept separated in a complicated system of pipes, valves, and pumps. On a typical voyage she might carry jet fuel, aviation gasoline, lubricating oil, stove oil, and automobile gasoline.

For me, the idyllic life was over. No more relaxed, single-product loading watches. Instead, I struggled to learn the intricate piping system. Things previously unknown to me became important: loading se-

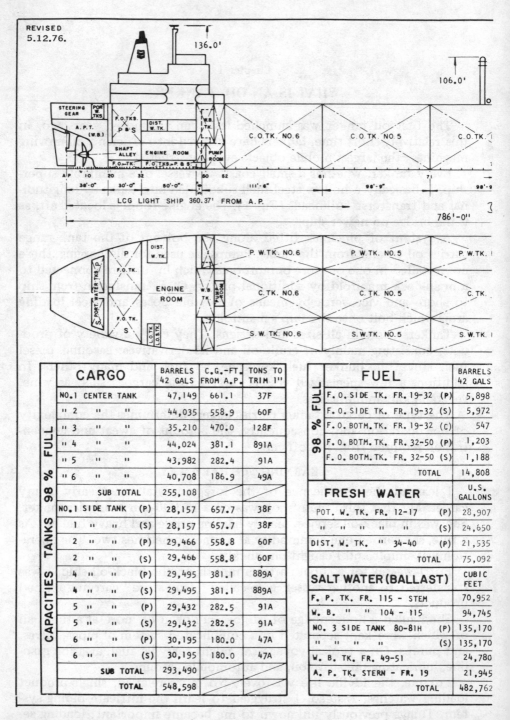

REVISED 5.12.76.

CARGO	BARRELS 42 GALS	C.G.-FT. FROM A.P.	TONS TO TRIM 1"
NO.1 CENTER TANK	47,149	661.1	37F
" 2 " "	44,035	558.9	60F
" 3 " "	35,210	470.0	128F
" 4 " "	44,024	381.1	891A
" 5 " "	43,982	282.4	91A
" 6 " "	40,708	186.9	49A
SUB TOTAL	255,108		
NO.1 SIDE TANK (P)	28,157	657.7	38F
1 " " (S)	28,157	657.7	38F
2 " " (P)	29,466	558.8	60F
2 " " (S)	29,466	558.8	60F
4 " " (P)	29,495	381.1	889A
4 " " (S)	29,495	381.1	889A
5 " " (P)	29,432	282.5	91A
5 " " (S)	29,432	282.5	91A
6 " " (P)	30,195	180.0	47A
6 " " (S)	30,195	180.0	47A
SUB TOTAL	293,490		
TOTAL	548,598		

98% FULL — CAPACITIES TANKS 98% FULL

FUEL	BARRELS 42 GALS
F.O. SIDE TK. FR. 19-32 (P)	5,898
F.O. SIDE TK. FR. 19-32 (S)	5,972
F.O. BOTM. TK. FR. 19-32 (C)	547
F.O. BOTM. TK. FR. 32-50 (P)	1,203
F.O. BOTM. TK. FR. 32-50 (S)	1,188
TOTAL	14,808

98% FULL

FRESH WATER	U.S. GALLONS
POT. W. TK. FR. 12-17 (P)	28,907
" " " " " (S)	24,650
DIST. W. TK. " 34-40 (P)	21,535
TOTAL	75,092

SALT WATER (BALLAST)	CUBIC FEET
F. P. TK. FR. 115 - STEM	70,952
W. B. " " 104 - 115	94,745
NO. 3 SIDE TANK 80-81H (P)	135,170
" " " " (S)	135,170
W. B. TK. FR. 49-51	24,780
A. P. TK. STERN - FR. 19	21,945
TOTAL	482,762

Fig. 1. General plan and particulars for the *Chevron Hawaii*, 70,000 d.w.t. Chevron Shipping Company.

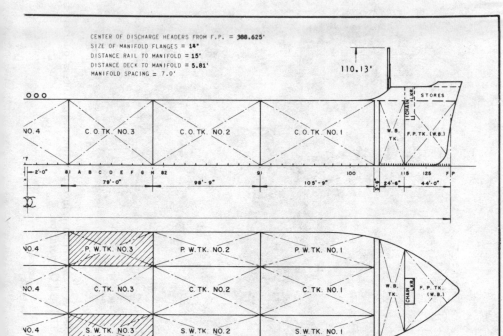

CENTER OF DISCHARGE HEADERS FROM F.P. = **388.625'**
SIZE OF MANIFOLD FLANGES = **14"**
DISTANCE RAIL TO MANIFOLD = **15'**
DISTANCE DECK TO MANIFOLD = **5.81'**
MANIFOLD SPACING = **7.0'**

C.G.-FT. FROM A.P.	TONS TO TRIM 1"
54.0	
54.0	29A
55.3	30A
101.6	34A
101.6	34A

C.G.-FT. FROM A.P.	TONS (2240LBS)
29.1	107
29.1	92
82.5	80
	279

C.G.-FT. FROM A.P.	TONS (2240LBS)
757.4	2,028
729.1	2,707
470.0	3,862
470.0	3,862
126.1	708
22.27	627
	13,794

MACHINERY

ENGINE – GENERAL ELECTRIC DOUBLE REDUCTION GEAR, CROSS COMPOUND STEAM TURBINE.
MAX: 20,000 SHP U.S. @ 112 RPM

BOILER – TWO FOSTER WHEELER 2-DRUM, OIL FIRED WATER TUBE MARINE BOILERS.
600 PSIG – 905°F

PARTICULARS

LENGTH	(O.A.)	810.00'
LENGTH	(B.P.)	786.00'
BREADTH	(MLD)	105.00'
DEPTH	(MLD)	57.00'
GROSS TON		35,588.74
NET TON		29,437
PANAMA GROSS TON		40,319
PANAMA NET TON		31,731.15

INTERNATIONAL LOAD LINES A B S

	DRAFT	DISP'MT	DEAD'WT	FREE'BD
LIGHT SHIP	3.88' FWD. 13.78 AFT.	14,877	—	—
ASSIGNED SUMMER	43.51'	85,090	70,213	13.73'
TROPICAL	44.41'	87,060	72,183	12.83'
WINTER	42.61'	83,210	68,333	14.62'
FRESH WATER ALLOWANCE	12.50	—	—	—

S/S CHEVRON HAWAII

OWNER .... UNION BANK
OPERATOR .... STANDARD OIL CO. OF CALIFORNIA
BUILDER .... BETHLEHEM STEEL CORP. SPARROWS POINT, M.D.
DELIVERY .... JUNE 28, 1973

OFFICIAL NO. 549197   HULL NO. 4638   CALL SIGN KNFD

Fig. 1. *(cont.)*

Fig. 2. Cutaway diagram of the *Gulfking*, a 30,000-d.w.t. tanker built in 1956. A forward house, incorporating deck officers' quarters and bridge, typifies older construction. Gulf Oil Corporation.

quence, cargo compatibility, bottom flushes, jumper hoses, two-valve separation, and more. In plain words, the operation of my first two ships could not have been more different.

THREE TYPES OF TANKERS

As my own experience illustrates, tankers logically fall into two categories, black-oil carriers and light-oil carriers. However, for the purposes of this book it is convenient to break them down further into three main groups: 1) crude carriers; 2) black-oil product carriers; 3) light-oil product carriers.

There is no sharp dividing line between these groups. In fact a vessel might serve in all three capacities during her lifetime: hauling crude, black-oil products, and light-oil products.

What marks a ship for a particular kind of service? Size is a vital factor. Given the wide range of sizes in today's tankers, it is convenient to classify them according to their carrying capacity, normally referred to as *deadweight tonnage*. This is the amount of cargo, fuel, water, and stores a vessel can carry when fully loaded. It is abbreviated *d.w.t.* and is expressed in long tons of 2,240 pounds each.

Table 1 separates tankers into three broad categories according to size. As the table indicates, product carriers are rarely designed to carry more than 35,000 tons deadweight. Crude carriers, on the other hand, are much bigger.

Table 1

THREE BROAD CLASSIFICATIONS OF TANKERS ACCORDING TO SIZE

Category	Tonnage Range	Type of Service
Handy or Small-Size Tankers	6,000— 35,000 d.w.t.	mainly product carriers
Medium-Size Tankers	35,000— 160,000 d.w.t.	mainly crude; heavy fuel oils on occasion
Very Large Crude Carriers	160,000 d.w.t. and above	crude exclusively

Plans have been drawn for a crude carrier of *one million* deadweight tons, and it is generally agreed that such a vessel could be built. However, because of the recent decrease in demand for tankers, these plans have been shelved, probably for good.

Any tanker in black-oil service can carry crude, and many smaller ships alternate between crude oil and the "dirty" distillates of crude such as bunker fuel. This practice is especially common on American coastwise tankers.

In contrast, light-oil ships rarely change over to crude or dirty products. When a ship's tanks have been contaminated by black oil, she

Fig. 3. With 1.8 million barrels of Persian Gulf crude in her tanks, the 253,000-d.w.t. VLCC *T.G. Shaughnessy* maneuvers alongside a dock in Nova Scotia. A smaller tanker loads refined products at an inner berth. Gulf Oil Corporation.

must either remain in black-oil service or undergo an expensive and time-consuming process of tank cleaning.

For this reason, tanker companies prefer to keep their ships in either black oil or light oil exclusively, changing over only on rare occasions.

CHANGES IN TANKER DESIGN SINCE WORLD WAR II

World War II accelerated the tanker's development and in so doing precipitated important changes. Prior to the war the typical tanker was powered by a diesel or reciprocating steam engine—speed, about 10 knots. She was tiny by today's standards. Her pumproom, located amidships, was fitted with steamdriven reciprocating pumps. These were sturdy, but slow.

A new class of tanker, the T2, was developed and mass produced during the war (Fig. 6). It soon became the backbone of the American fleet. At 16,500 d.w.t., the T2 was considered a big ship in its day. The pumproom, located aft, incorporated three centrifugal pumps and a direct pipeline system. These speeded up cargo handling significantly.

In the intervening years other changes have taken place. Tankers are bigger. The midship house, home of the deck officers and bridge for so many years, has disappeared. Virtually all new tankers are "stern-winders" fitted with a single house aft (Fig. 7).

The reciprocating steam engine has faded into the history books. Today's typical tanker is powered by a steam turbine connected to the propeller shaft by reduction gears. This type of propulsion has proven especially adaptable to very large ships.

Some tankers are fitted with diesel engines but this is rare under the American flag. Other types of propulsion such as gas turbines have also been used successfully on smaller vessels (Fig. 8).

Automation. Most new tankers are at least partially automated. For example, cargo operations are often monitored and controlled from a console in the cargo control room. Hydraulic valves inside the tanks are opened and closed remotely.

Computers play an important role on some vessels and a few are virtually computer-controlled; that is, cargo operations, navigation, and engine operation can all be controlled automatically by computer. In addition, computers can be programmed to handle routine administrative chores, such as crew's wages. Or, in an emergency, a computer might offer an accurate medical diagnosis complete with suggested treatment for a sick crew member.

Automation is not the rule, however, on the many older—and usually smaller—tankers still in service throughout the world. Some are partially automated; many others are not automated at all.

VLCCs

Very Large Crude Carriers, or VLCCs, can be defined roughly as tankers of 160,000 d.w.t. and over. They have been joined recently by

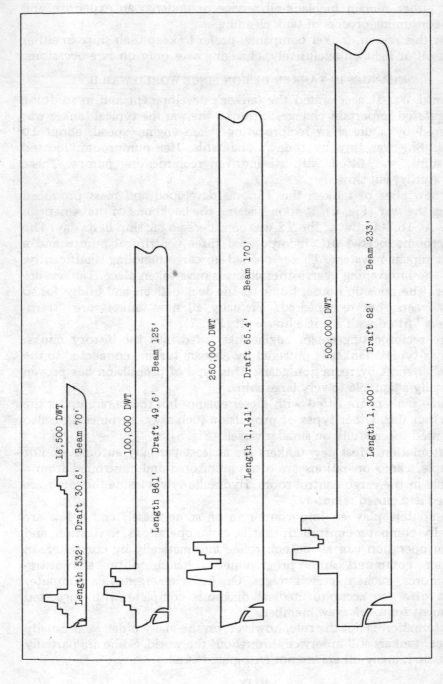

Fig. 4. This diagram shows the relative sizes of tankers. The size of tankers has increased dramatically since World War II. The first figure represents a T2. Exxon Corporation.

Length 532'   Draft 30.6'   Beam 70'
16,500 DWT

Length 861'   Draft 49.6'   Beam 125'
100,000 DWT

Length 1,141'   Draft 65.4'   Beam 170'
250,000 DWT

Length 1,300'   Draft 82'   Beam 233'
500,000 DWT

Fig. 5. The *K.R. Kingsbury,* 12,000 d.w.t., was launched in 1921. Bethlehem Ship-building Company Collection, San Francisco Maritime Museum.

Fig. 6. A T2 tanker, 16,500 d.w.t., makes her final voyage to lay-up. Designed and built during World War II, the T2s were considered big ships in their day. U.S. Maritime Administration.

Fig. 7. The *Sansinena II*, 70,000 d.w.t. Bethlehem Steel Corporation.

a newer class of ships: *Ultra* Large Crude Carriers, or ULCCs (tankers over 400,000 d.w.t.). VLCCs and ULCCs are the largest moving objects ever built by man.

Like lonely giants spurned by the world, these ships roam the most solitary trade routes ever known to seafarers. They are so huge that few harbors can receive them.

Fig. 8. The *Chevron Washington*, 35,000 d.w.t., is powered by gas-turbine/electric drive. Ackroyd Photography, Inc., and FMC Corporation.

A typical voyage might begin at an isolated loading platform in the Persian Gulf. The ship loads quickly and begins her long voyage (perhaps a month or more) to the receiving terminal. This is usually a lonely dock or an offshore mooring far from civilization.

Here the ship discharges her cargo in a matter of hours and, after filling up with saltwater ballast, starts the long return voyage to the Gulf—an unending odyssey.

As a rule, VLCCs are built in foreign yards and rarely fly the American flag. There are exceptions, however (Fig. 10).

At present few American terminals can accommodate ships of more than 70,000 d.w.t. However, plans are currently underway for the construction of several "superports" off the coast of the United States. Two of these, both in the Gulf of Mexico, have already been approved by the government.

Fig. 9. Main engine room control console on board the 215,000-d.w.t. VLCC *British Explorer*. Photo by The British Petroleum Co. Ltd.

ORE/BULK/OIL CARRIERS

Ore/Bulk/Oil Carriers, or OBOs, are specially built tankers capable of carrying bulk commodities such as ore and coal. Many are in the VLCC class. On an ideal voyage an OBO carries oil in one direction, ore or coal in the other. Revenue is thus earned each way.

When tanker demand decreases, charter rates go down—often to unprofitable levels (as they did following the Middle Eastern War of 1973). In such situations the OBO demonstrates her most valuable attribute—versatility. She simply switches to ore or coal until freight rates for oil return to a profitable level. She thus continues to earn revenue while other tankers sit idle.

The design of an OBO is necessarily different from that of a regular tanker. The center tanks are wider and are fitted with large hatches on the main deck (Fig. 11). The center-tank bottoms are built with an inward slope toward the keel for more efficient stowage of non-oil cargoes.

When carrying oil, both center and wing tanks can be used for cargo stowage (although the wings are reserved for ballast on some vessels). Only the centers are used when carrying ore, coal, etc.

LNG CARRIERS

Natural gas—composed mainly of methane—exists in abundance in most oil fields, either dissolved in the crude itself or wedged between it and the earth's surface. When an oil field is tapped, natural gas is released.

Unfortunately, this gas must often be flared, or burned off, because no means is available for transporting it to consumers.

But the situation is changing. The demand for efficient, clean-burning fuels has led to the development of a new class of ship, the LNG (liquefied natural gas) Carrier (Fig. 12). These ships are designed to carry natural gas at extremely low temperatures—on the order of -260° F. (-162° C.)—thus keeping it liquefied.

It follows that LNG Carriers must be carefully insulated. To accomplish this, a variety of designs are used. For example, one popular design incorporates spherical cargo tanks made from aluminum alloy; these are insulated with polyurethane.

Because no refrigeration system is used on ships carrying LNG, a certain amount of cargo boils off each voyage and is lost. Most LNG Carriers use at least part of this boiloff as fuel in their own boilers.

A closed system is used when loading and discharging LNG. Specially constructed flow booms are connected between ship and shore; these carry the liquid cargo. A *vapor boom* is also connected. This serves as a vent line between ship and shore.

When loading, for example, vaporized natural gas is vented ashore. When discharging, the gas is vented from shore tanks to the ship.

As a rule, a small amount of LNG is retained on board after discharging. This keeps the tanks cold for the next load.

Fig. 10. The *Brooklyn*, American-flag VLCC (225,000 d.w.t.). U.S. Maritime Administration.

Fig. 11. The *Jag Leela*, 136,000-d.w.t. Ore/Bulk/Oil Carrier. Kockums Automation AB.

Fig. 12. A modern LNG Carrier. Capacity: 125,000 cubic meters (64,000 d.w.t.). General Dynamics Corporation.

Chapter 2

HOW OIL IS MEASURED AND CLASSIFIED

A new officer reports aboard his first tanker. Suitcase in hand, he stands outside the chief mate's office. The door is open; inside a middle-aged man in khaki overalls works busily at some paperwork. The new man steps inside and puts his suitcase down.

"Are you the chief mate?"

"Yes," the man in overalls says, without looking up.

"I'm John Smith, the new third mate."

"Smith? Fine, just in time to get the gauges."

"The what?"

"Gauges—ullage readings—so we can figure the amount of oil on board. You know how to do it?"

Smith hesitates. "Well, I have a general idea but I've never seen it done."

The chief mate hands Smith a clipboard. "Here. See what you can come up with."

BASIC KNOWLEDGE

As the foregoing illustrates, cargo gauging—ullaging—is one of the first things a new officer must learn. The techniques used are simple, but they must be mastered thoroughly and performed meticulously. It is wise to gain an understanding of these techniques before setting foot on a tanker.

The first step in the ullaging process is to take the ullages themselves; we will discuss how this is done shortly. With this information, the following can be ascertained: 1) gross barrels of cargo; 2) net barrels of cargo; 3) tonnage of cargo; 4) loading/discharging rate.

A tanker is ullaged each time she arrives in port; this is also done just before sailing. The ullages are recorded on forms (Fig. 13), which are then distributed to ship, terminal, and main office of the vessel's owner or charterer. Ullages are also taken at intervals during the loading or discharging operation as a means of determining the amount of cargo on board at a given time.

UNITS OF MEASURE

The following units of measure are used on American tankers:

1 barrel = 42 gallons
1 ton = 2,240 pounds
1 net barrel = 42 gallons (adjusted to 60° F.)
1 gross barrel = 42 gallons (at actual temperature in tank)

16

These units are used in conjunction with the following formulas:

net barrels = gross barrels x M
(where M is a multiplier taken from the Pretroleum Tables)

$$\text{tons} = \frac{\text{net barrels}}{\text{barrels per ton}}$$

However, the American barrel and long ton by no means constitute a universal standard. For example, British tankers are calibrated in cubic feet. Some other nations use liters and metric tons (1 metric ton = 1,000 kilograms = 2,204.6 pounds). The gallon may also be encountered on very small ships. Different stowage factors are also used, to match volumetric units: cubic feet per ton, liters per metric ton, pounds per gallon, etc.

Table 2

EXTRACT FROM CARGO TANK CALIBRATION TABLE

San Clemente Class Tanker

No. 1 Wing Tanks

ullage	barrels	cubic feet
5′ 00″	28,312	158,972
1″	28,269	158,730
2″	28,225	158,483
3″	28,181	158,236
4″	28,137	157,989
5″	28,093	157,742
6″	28,049	157,495
7″	28,005	157,248
8″	27,961	157,001
9″	27,918	156,760
10″	27,874	156,513
11″	27,830	156,265
6′ 00″	27,786	156,018

These differences are superficial. Regardless of the units employed, the same basic techniques are used to ullage tankers throughout the world. Master these techniques and you will have little difficulty making the transition from an American ship to one of foreign registry, or vice versa.

GAUGING THE SHIP

When a tanker is new, each tank is calibrated and a set of tables prepared; these indicate cargo volume at various ullages (see Table 2). Ullage (often referred to as *outage* on board ship) is the distance from an above-deck datum (the top of the ullage hole, in most cases) to the surface of the oil in the tank (Fig. 14).

On American and British tankers this distance is measured in feet and inches; a number of other nations use meters. Ullages are often measured by automatic tape on American vessels, and a few ships are

(Text continues on page 22.)

Ullage Report

Dock		Ship	
Port	Incoming cargo	Voyage number	
	Outgoing cargo	Date	Time

Tank No.	Grade	Ullage		Inches	Trim adjustment	Adjust ullage		Gross bbls.	Temp.	Net 60° bbls.	Water	
		Feet	Inches			Feet	Inches				Inches	Bbls.

Port												
1					+1½″	5			66			
2												
3												
4												
5												
6												
7												
8												
9												
10												
11												
Starboard												
1												
2												
3												
4												
5												

(Tank numbers go up to eleven)

Fig. 13. Ullage report form. Atlantic Richfield Company.

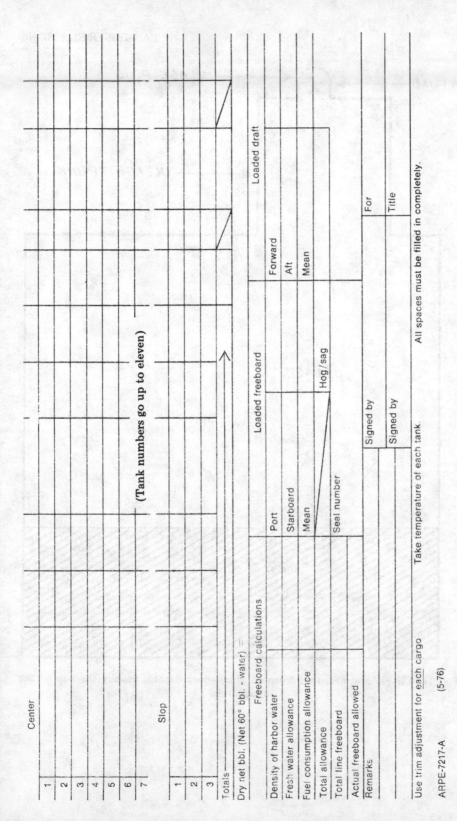

Fig. 13. (cont.)

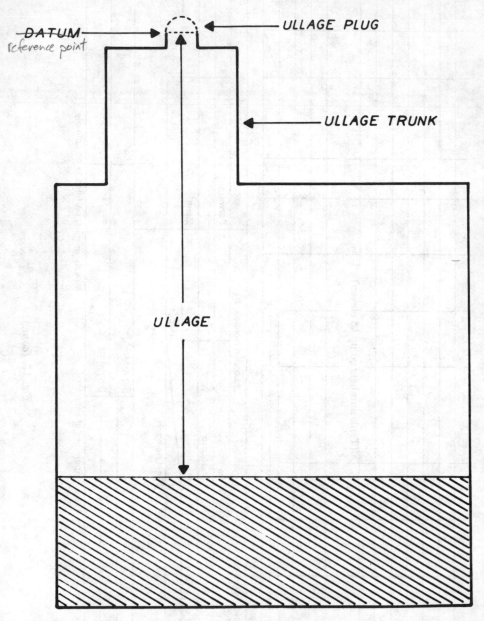

Fig. 14. Ullages are measured from an above-deck datum, usually the top of the ullage hole.

reference depth = outage + inage

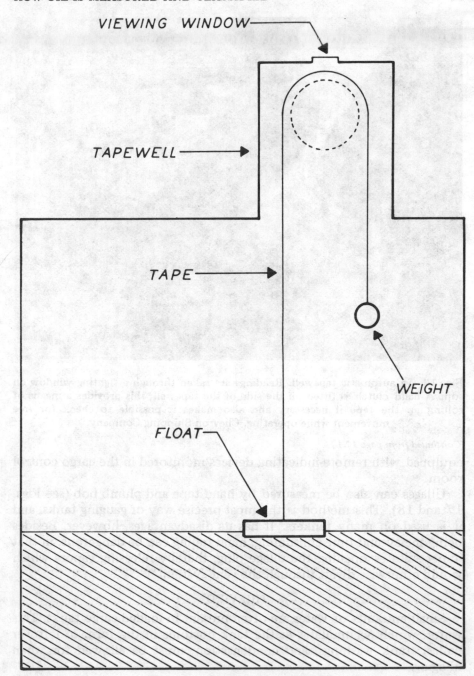

Fig. 15. How an automatic tape works.

Fig. 16. An automatic tapewell. Readings are taken through a sighting window on top. A hand clutch is fitted on the side of the tapewell; this provides a means of rolling up the tape if necessary and also makes it possible to check for free movement while operating. Chevron Shipping Company.

(Continued from page 17.)

equipped with remote-indicating devices monitored in the cargo control room.

Ullages can also be measured by hand tape and plumb bob (see Figs. 17 and 18). This method is the most precise way of gauging tanks, and it is used on many tankers. It has its disadvantages, however. Besides being messy and time-consuming, hand taping can be dangerous, in that it necessitates opening the ullage plug, thereby releasing vapors which would otherwise divert through the vent system.

THIEVING

Small amounts of water are often present in loaded cargo tanks. This water—which accumulates at the tank bottoms in the form of leftover ballast, tank washings, and condensation—must be allowed for when ullaging.

A process called *thieving* is employed for this purpose. A graduated metal rod is smeared with litmus paste (which changes color when contacted by water but isn't affected by oil). The rod is lowered until it touches bottom, then is retrieved. The amount of water at the bottom of the tank is determined by noting the place on the graduated rod where the paste changes color.

GROSS BARRELS

After each tank has been ullaged and (if necessary) thieved, the calibration tables are entered to determine gross barrels.

The first step is to correct the ullages for trim. As a rule, this must be done if the vessel is trimmed a foot or more by the head or stern. Trim corrections are most often found on a separate page of the calibration tables (see Table 3). Corrections are given in inches or fractions of an inch for various conditions of trim; these must be added to, or subtracted from, the observed ullages.

Table 3

S.S. ATLANTIC ROVER

Trim Corrections
(in inches)

trim by the stern

Tank	1′	2′	3′	4′	5′	6′	7′	8′	9′
1C	+½	+½	+1	+1	+1½	+1½	+1½	+2	+2
2C	----	----	+½	+½	+1	+1	+1	+1½	+1½
3C	----	+½	+½	+1	+1	+1½	+1½	+2	+2
4C	----	----	−½	−½	−1	−1	−1½	−1½	−2
5C	----	+½	+½	+½	+1	+1	+1½	+1½	+1½
6C	----	+½	+½	+½	+1	+1	+1½	+1½	+1½
1P	+½	+½	+1	+1	+1½	+1½	+1½	+2	+2
1S	+½	+½	+1	+1	+1½	+1½	+1½	+2	+2
2P	----	----	+½	+½	+1	+1	+1	+1½	+1½
2S	----	----	+½	+½	+1	+1	+1	+1½	+1½
3P	----	+½	+½	+1	+1	+1½	+1½	+2	+2
3S	----	+½	+½	+1	+1	+1½	+1½	+2	+2
4P	----	----	−½	−1	−1	−1½	−1½	−2	−2
4S	----	----	−½	−½	−1	−1	−1½	−1½	−2
5P	----	+½	+½	+½	+1	+1	+1½	+1½	+1½
5S	----	+½	+½	+½	+1	+1	+1½	+1½	+1½
6P	----	+½	+½	+1	+1	+1½	+1½	+2	+2
6S	----	+½	+½	+1	+1	+1½	+1½	+2	+2

Apply corrections to observed ullages.

After correcting each reading, the main part of the calibration tables is entered and the number of gross barrels corresponding to each ullage is noted. These values are listed for given intervals of ullage (every inch, for example). Depending on desired accuracy, some interpolation may be necessary; this can be done by inspection.

The sum of these figures yields the total number of gross barrels on board.

Fig. 17. Ullaging with a hand tape. Chevron Shipping Company.

NET BARRELS

All petroleum products have an important characteristic in common—they expand when heated, contract when cooled. For this reason petroleum engineers have established a standard temperature from which to calculate the net amount of oil in a tank. This temperature is 60° F. (15.6° C.).

Table 4

SAMPLE API AND SPECIFIC GRAVITIES

Product	API	Specific Gravity
Motor Gasoline	61.0	.7351
Kerosene	49.0	.7839
Gas Oil	39.0	.8299
Benzine	29.0	.8816
Bunker Fuel	15.0	.9659
Heavy Fuel Oil	9.5	1.0035

Determining net barrels is a simple matter of multiplying gross barrels by a multiplier obtained from the Petroleum Tables (see Tables 5A & 5B). Entering arguments are temperature and API gravity.

Cargo temperature is ascertained either by direct immersion of a thermometer or by observing an average temperature as cargo passes

Fig. 18. Hand taping is sometimes used to check the accuracy of automatic readings. Photo by The British Petroleum Co. Ltd.

through the manifold (which is equipped with built-in thermometers for this purpose). Although less precise, the latter method is preferred, because it is faster and less messy. It also avoids the opening of ullage plugs and resultant escape of hazardous vapors.

Table 5A

EXTRACT FROM THE PETROLEUM TABLES

Multipliers for Group 2 (35.0 to 50.9° API @ 60° F.)

Temperature	Multiplier
54	1.0030
55	1.0025
56	1.0020
57	1.0015
58	1.0010
59	1.0005
60	1.0000
61	.9995
62	.9990
63	.9985
64	.9980
65	.9975
66	.9970

API gravity is nothing more than a convenient way of expressing the specific gravity of a product. An arbitrary gravity of 10.0° is assigned to fresh water. Numbers above 10.0° indicate products lighter than fresh water; those below, heavier. Light products such as gasoline have API values considerably greater than 10.0°, while a few products such as heavy fuel oil have values less than 10.0°.

A glance at Table 4 shows that API gravity is easily converted to specific gravity, and vice versa. This is a helpful conversion, because ships of some nations (Great Britain, for example) use specific gravity instead of API.

It is possible to measure API and specific gravities on board ship, but the preferred practice is to use a figure provided by shoreside personnel. There are two good reasons for this. First, shoreside facilities and methods are more precise. Second, the use of one figure prevents discrepancies between shoreside and shipboard figures.

When API gravity and cargo temperature are both known, it is a simple matter to extract the multiplier from the Petroleum Tables. Simply enter the tables for the appropriate group and pick out the multiplier for the corresponding temperature. This number, when multiplied by gross barrels, gives the desired figure for net barrels.

TONNAGE

The ship's officers—particularly the chief mate—must frequently compute cargo tonnages. Tonnages are especially important when figuring draft, trim, displacement, and stress.

Table 5B

EXTRACT FROM THE PETROLEUM TABLES

API, Specific Gravity, and Barrels per Ton

API Gravity	Specific Gravity	42-Gallon Bbls. per Long Ton
24.4	.9076	7.056
24.5	.9071	7.061
24.6	.9065	7.066
24.7	.9059	7.070
24.8	.9053	7.075
24.9	.9047	7.079
25.0	.9042	7.084
25.1	.9036	7.088
25.2	.9030	7.093
25.3	.9024	7.097
25.4	.9018	7.102
25.5	.9013	7.106
25.6	.9007	7.111

To determine the tonnage of a given product, enter the appropriate section of the Petroleum Tables. Pick out the barrels per ton; this corresponds to the API gravity of the product (see Table 5B). The tonnage is equal to net barrels divided by barrels per ton.

Let's illustrate with an example.

A parcel of bunker fuel is loaded, and the following information is known:

gross barrels = 125,432
temperature = 125° F.
API gravity = 14.0

How many net barrels, and how many tons, of bunker fuel were loaded?

The first step in the solution is to enter the Petroleum Tables, from which the following information is taken:

M = .9775
barrels per ton = 6.585

With this information the necessary calculations can be made:

.9775 x 125,432 = 122,610 net barrels

$\frac{122,610}{6.585}$ = 18,620 tons

LOADING AND DISCHARGING RATES

Loading and discharging rates vary considerably for different ships, different terminals, and different cargoes. For example, a VLCC might load 60,000 barrels per hour (8,000 tons per hour) at a terminal in the Persian Gulf, while a small product carrier might load less than 1,000 barrels per hour at an American refinery.

Some of the factors which influence rates are: number and size of pumps, size of shore lines, temperature and viscosity of cargo, number of tanks open, and distance from shore tanks to ship.

In order to gain some idea of when the cargo will finish, the officer on watch must figure the loading rate at periodic intervals, usually every one or two hours. This procedure is a routine part of each cargo watch; it is therefore important to understand it thoroughly.

On American ships rates are measured in barrels per hour (British vessels use tons per hour). The process is simple, as is explained in the following paragraphs.

Gauge the ship at periodic intervals (you may ignore trim corrections when gauging for rate); determine the total cargo on board; find the difference between this figure and the last total; divide this difference by the number of hours elapsed between these measurements. The result is the rate in barrels per hour.

To determine estimated time of finish, divide the barrels to go by the rate; this will give hours to go. Figure 19 shows a typical form for computing loading rates. A similar form is used when discharging.

FLAMMABLE AND COMBUSTIBLE LIQUIDS

A wide variety of petroleum products are shipped by sea, from the

S.S. SHASTA VALLEY
Loading Rates

Total gross barrels: 447,000   Date: 7-21-77

Start @ 0400

	0600	0800	1000	1200	1400	1600
1C	5422	10,598	10,598	10,598	10,598	
2C	7526	15,105	23,987	34,299	43,290	
3C	MT	MT	MT	MT	MT	MT
4C	8312	16,678	26,390	36,793	43,278	
5C	9746	19,471	30,517	43,236	43,236	
6C	10,224	20,550	32,130	39,987	39,987	
1P					2681	
S					2681	
2P					3191	
S					3240	
4P					3235	
S					3235	
6P					3786	
S					3742	
Aboard:	41,230	82,402	123,622	164,913	206,180	
To Go:	405,770	364,598	323,378	282,087	240,820	
Rate:	20,615	20,586	20,610	20,646	20,634	
Est. Finish:	0145 7-22-77	0145	0145	0145	0145	

Fig. 19. A typical form for computing loading rates.

crudes and residual fuels carried on black-oil tankers to the gasoline, jet
fuel, and lubricating oil carried on light-oil tankers.

Table 6

GRADES OF PETROLEUM PRODUCTS

Grade	Flash Point	Reid Vapor Pressure	Examples
A (flammable)	80° F. or below	14 psi or above	natural gasoline, very light naphthas
B (flammable)	80° F. or below	more than 8½ psi but less than 14 psi	most commercial gasolines
C (flammable)	80° F. or below	8½ psi or below	most crude oils, creosote, aviation gas grade 115/145, JP-4 jet fuel
D (combustible)	above 80° F. but below 150° F.	——	kerosene, some heavy crudes, commercial jet fuels
E (combustible)	150° F. or above	——	heavy fuel oils, lubricating oils, asphalt

Nearly all are flammable. Some, like gasoline, are extremely
flammable while others, like lubricating oil, are relatively safe. The
more flammable substances require special precautions and, for this
reason, petroleum products are graded according to their volatility
(Table 6). They are divided into two main groups:

1. **Flammable liquids** are those which give off flammable vapors at or
below 80° F. (26.7° C.). These are further subdivided into grades A, B,
and C on the basis of their Reid Vapor Pressure (a measurement of
vapor given off in a closed container heated to 100° F.).

2. **Combustible liquids** are those which give off flammable vapors at
temperatures above 80° F.

Fig. 20. Sailors connect a loading arm to the riser of a 215,000-ton VLCC at Europoort, the Netherlands. Photo by The British Petroleum Co. Ltd.

Chapter 3

CARGO PIPING SYSTEMS

It is a sunny, cloudless day in Sydney, Australia. A freighter glides into port, maneuvers alongside the wharf, and within a few minutes is safely docked. Longshore gangs swarm aboard and crew members saunter ashore for a night on the town.

At the same time, thousands of miles away in Cook Inlet, Alaska, another ship—a tanker—is being carefully maneuvered through a snowstorm. She makes fast to an isolated platform far out in the inlet, her crew bolts the platform's loading arm to the ship's manifold, and crude oil begins to pour aboard at 20,000 barrels per hour. No one comes aboard; no one leaves.

These examples, although hypothetical, dramatize an important point, *i.e.*, freighters and tankers differ profoundly.

A cargo watch on a freighter can be a boisterous, disorganized affair involving dozens of people. The ship's officers have little control over the actual operation. But a tanker is different. Quietly and efficiently, a handful of crew members guide the oil into the ship by opening a valve here, closing one there. They are in complete control.

Of course, any freighter mate worth his salt should have a good working knowledge of the complex maze of booms, guys, topping lifts, and other rigging used for cargo handling. A tanker mate, on the other hand, *must* know the cargo piping system of his ship. The operation rests on his shoulders, and his alone.

THE DIRECT PIPELINE SYSTEM

Most modern tankers are fitted with a direct pipeline system for handling cargo. Simply stated, the tanks are divided into groups, or systems, with a different pump and line for each system.

Figure 21 diagrams a direct pipeline arrangement for an 18-tank ship. The system incorporates three main cargo pumps, each handling two tanks across (that is, two center tanks and four wing tanks). Figure 22 illustrates another possible arrangement for the same ship. This time only two pumps are fitted—one for centers, one for wings.

In both cases a separate line runs from each pump along the bottom of the tank range to the tanks in its system. Shorter sections of pipe branch off from the main lines to each individual tank.

These pipelines vary in diameter from 10-12 inches (25-30 cm.) on handy-size tankers to 36 inches (91 cm.) on VLCCs.

31

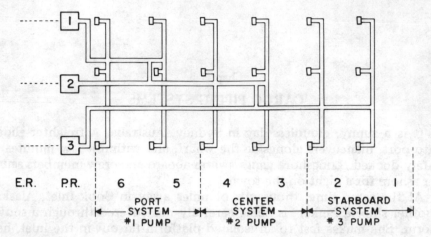

Fig. 21. Direct pipeline system incorporating three lines and three pumps. Crossovers are provided between systems (no valves are shown). Bill Finhandler.

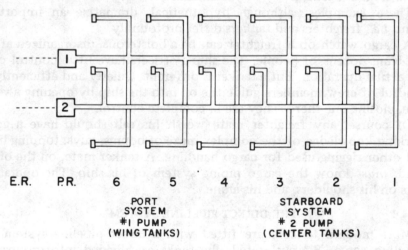

Fig. 22. Direct pipeline system incorporating two lines and two pumps. Center tanks are on one system, wing tanks on the other. Bill Finhandler.

LEARNING THE CARGO SYSTEM

As a new officer you should strive to learn these cargo systems quickly. In addition, you should know the location and purpose of the following:

Tank valves. The main pipeline carries oil along the bottom of the tank range. Along the way it connects to branch lines, one per tank. At the end of each branch line the piping spreads into a *bellmouth*, an arrangement which resembles a large vacuum cleaner (see Fig. 52, Chapter 5). This allows suction to be taken close to the bottom of the tank.

Fig. 23. Loading arms are secured with bolted flanges or special hydraulic fittings.
An Exxon Photo.

In addition, a tank valve is fitted near the end of the branch line. This valve is operated in one of two ways: 1) automatically, from the cargo control room; 2) manually, from the deck above.

While an increasing number of ships have been fitted with automatic valves, many still use manual control. And here a question arises: How do you operate a valve which lies deep within a cargo tank—perhaps 50 feet below the main deck—and is frequently submerged in oil?

To make tank valve operation possible, a metal reach rod connects each valve stem to a handwheel on the main deck. One turn of the handwheel produces a corresponding turn on the valve inside the tank.

The handwheel is fitted with a threaded indicator, called a *telltale*, which travels from "open" to "closed" as the valve is turned (see Fig. 35, Chapter 4). One caution: Telltales sometimes stick, jam, or become stripped, thus causing an incorrect reading.

Drops. Cargo is loaded through filling lines called drops. These are located on each line in the pumproom and at various locations on the main deck. Each drop is equipped with a valve; this must be open when loading through that line. While discharging, drop valves are kept closed to prevent cargo from recirculating to the tanks.

Line drops route cargo into the underdeck piping system; therefore, individual tank valves must still be opened before cargo can enter the tanks.

Fig. 24. A tanker's manifold, or "riser." Pipelines are blanked off when not in use. A fixed drip pan catches leaks from flanged couplings. An Exxon Photo.

A *tank drop*, on the other hand, serves a single tank; oil bypasses the main piping system and flows directly into the tank. Tank drops are more apt to be found on ships carrying refined cargoes, where the need for separation makes it desirable to bypass the main system.

Crossovers. The various systems are connected by sections of pipe known as crossovers. Each crossover is fitted with a valve, or valves,(↑ isolatn) thus making it possible to isolate the systems or link them together, as desired.

When loading the same product in all tanks, as on a crude carrier, crossovers are generally opened to allow cargo to flow freely through all systems. In the case of differing products, as on a product carrier, crossovers must be closed to prevent mixing.

Master valves. At each place where the bottom piping passes through a bulkhead and enters the next tank, a valve is fitted in the line. This is a master valve. Master valves provide separation between tanks on the same line and make it possible to isolate a single tank completely.

Manifold. Cargo flows from ship to shore, and vice versa, through flexible hoses or hinged loading arms which bolt to the ship's manifold, or "riser" (Fig. 24). By means of various valves built into the manifold, cargo can be routed to line drops along the main deck or to the pump-room—or to both simultaneously. The manifold is also equipped with pressure gauges and thermometers for each line.

When learning the cargo systems, you should memorize which systems tie into each manifold line (that is, which tanks and pumps are commonly tied into a given manifold outlet). Note the location of crossovers between manifold lines and observe how these are used to route cargo between systems.

Pumproom. The pumproom is the Grand Central Station of an oil tanker; all pipelines meet and interconnect in a relatively small area, usually located aft of the cargo tanks.

You should study the pumproom carefully. Learn the systems each pump is connected to, plus the designation for each pump (such as, number 1 main cargo pump, starboard stripper, etc.).

Learn the location and purpose of every valve, including crossover, drop, pump suction, pump discharge, sea suction, and block valves to each main and stripping line. Locate all vent cocks and line drains.

(You might try going over the entire piping system each night as you lie in bed. Try to visualize each valve, especially the important ones like crossovers and drops. This learning method works very well for me.)

The pumproom diagram—usually posted in the chief mate's office—is a valuable tool. However, there is no substitute for climbing through the pumproom and seeing each valve. Ask yourself questions while doing this: *With this valve open and this one closed, which path will the oil follow?*

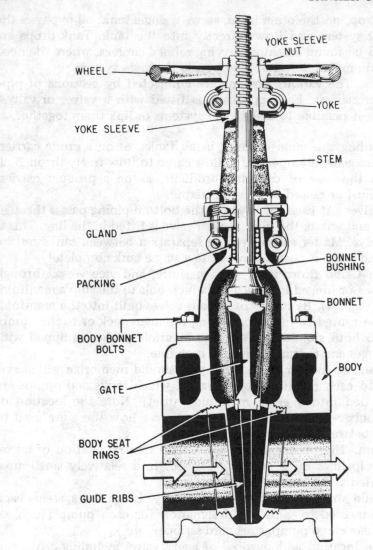

YOKE SLEEVE NUT

WHEEL

YOKE

YOKE SLEEVE

STEM

GLAND

BONNET BUSHING

PACKING

BONNET

BODY BONNET BOLTS

BODY

GATE

BODY SEAT RINGS

GUIDE RIBS

Fig. 25. Gate valve. U.S. Coast Guard.

Follow and observe the pumpman when he changes the lineup. Ask him to explain what he's doing. Then, when you are confident you know the system, line it up yourself. Have the chief mate or pumpman check your work.

While exploring the pumproom, you will notice that drops are fitted into each line. As we have already learned, these make it possible to load through the pumproom. However, it is often preferable to isolate the pumproom while loading, and to bypass it by routing cargo through line drops on the main deck.

To accomplish this, upper and lower master and block valves are closed at the pumproom bulkhead, thus sealing it off from the rest of the cargo system. This practice is common when loading heavy crudes and fuel oils which might clog the intricate piping system of the pumproom.

Stripping system. Many ships use a separate stripping system to pump out the last few barrels from each tank. Such systems employ reciprocating or other positive displacement pumps which are well suited to the task of draining tanks. Because they handle a relatively small amount of cargo, stripping lines, valves, and pumps are considerably smaller than those used on the main systems.

As a rule, main and stripping systems are kept separate, but crossovers make it possible to connect them if desired. Stripping pumps can therefore discharge or take suction through the main lines whenever necessary. (Some vessels use no stripping system whatsoever, except a small valve and a short branch line running from the main line in each tank. On these ships all stripping is done through the main line.)

TYPES OF VALVES

The cargo piping system of a typical tanker incorporates valves of various designs. These include:

Gate valves. As the name implies, this type of valve employs a metal gate, fitted in grooves, which slides across the valve opening (Fig. 25). The gate is fitted with a threaded spindle which connects to the valve stem. When turned by means of a handwheel, the spindle edges the gate slowly upward or downward.

It is necessary to turn the handwheel many times—perhaps 30 or more—to move the gate from fully open to fully closed. Gate valves are therefore too slow and cumbersome to be easily adapted to automatic control.

But they have advantages. They are dependable and durable. When fully open, the gate retracts into the valve body and offers no resistance to the flow of oil—a definite advantage over valves with swinging gates. In addition, gate valves provide an accurate adjustment to the rate of flow.

Butterfly valves. On tankers with automatic valve control, butterfly valves (Fig. 26) are commonly used instead of gate valves. They possess the following advantages:

1. They operate easily and quickly (¼ turn swings the gate from fully open to fully closed).

2. They adapt readily to automatic control.

3. They are more compact and less expensive than gate valves.

Butterfly valves have thus become standard equipment on ships with automated cargo control rooms. Hydraulic power—the only kind of power safe to use inside the tanks—gives pushbutton control to valve operation.

This arrangement is dictated by necessity on many large ships. First of all, the valves are so massive that manual operation is extremely difficult, if not impossible. Second, the vast distances between tanks makes local operation impractical.

Fig. 26. Butterfly valve. Valve Manufacturers Association.

Butterfly valves have several important disadvantages:

1. They fail to provide a precise adjustment to cargo flow; in most cases they must be operated fully open or fully closed.

2. The valve gate remains in the center of flow, even when fully open, thus offering resistance and slowing the rate.

3. Butterfly valves tend to develop leaks more readily and need more frequent maintenance than gate valves.

Globe valves are not as common in cargo systems as gate and butter-fly valves, but they are favored on some vessels.

A round disc is fitted on the end of a threaded stem. As the stem is turned with the handwheel, the disc wedges into the valve aperture, directly against the flow of oil. This action is a little like stopping a bottle with a cork.

Globe valves tend to be difficult to operate in large sizes and at high pressures, and because oil must change direction as it flows through the valve, an undesirable pressure drop may occur on the outlet side.

Nevertheless, globe valves are valuable whenever a precise throttling, or control of pressure, is desired.

Angle valves are basically globe valves in which the inlet and outlet flanges are turned at a 90-degree angle to each other, forming an elbow (Fig. 27).

Angle valves produce less resistance to flow than a globe-valve/elbow combination; they are therefore the economical choice when a valve is needed at a bend in a pipeline. Like globe valves, angle valves provide excellent throttling control in the partially open position.

SPECIAL VALVES

Certain valves perform special functions in the cargo system:

Check valves. To prevent oil from back-flowing into the tanks, a check valve is normally installed on the discharge side of each centrifugal pump.

Each valve contains a weighted or spring-loaded gate which swings up under pressure, allowing oil to flow out the discharge line. When the pump stops and pressure ceases, the gate swings shut against the valve seat, preventing oil from running back into the tanks.

Because check valves operate automatically, many officers tend to forget them or take them for granted. They are foolish to do so: check valves sometimes stick, causing spills when least expected.

You should never assume a check valve is working properly. Whenever the pumps are stopped, even temporarily, close the block valves at the manifold for sure protection against cargo backflow.

Relief valves. Each cargo pump is equipped with a relief valve and a short recirculating line. Whenever the pressure becomes excessive on the discharge side of the pump, the relief valve opens and allows oil to recirculate to the suction side, thereby relieving the pressure.

VALVE MARKINGS

On most tankers a system of one sort or another is used for marking valves and main-deck handwheels which operate valves inside the tanks. This practice reduces confusion and diminishes the risk of serious mistakes.

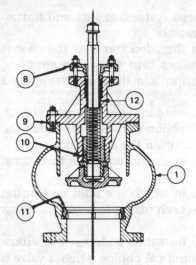

Flanges are 125 lbs. ANSI Dimensions.

REF. NO.	NO. PCS.	PART
1	1	BODY
2	1	BONNETT
3	1	STEM
4	1	BONNET BUSHING
5	1	LOCK NUT
6	1	LOCK WASHER
7	1	DISC
8	1	GLAND
9	1	GASKET
10	1	LOCK PIN
11	1	SEAT RING
12	1	GUIDE BUSHING
13	1	HANDWHEEL (NOT SHOWN)

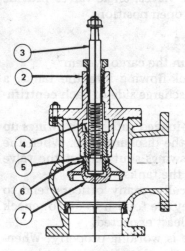

Fig. 27. Angle valve. Hayward Manufacturing Company.

Pumproom valves are often numbered; numbers are stencilled on each valve and are also indicated on a plan kept in the ship's office. Manifold valves are sometimes marked to indicate which pumping system each riser normally ties into (for example, *No. 1 pump—1, 2, 3, 4 across*).

The marking of handwheels on the main deck is especially helpful, because they operate valves remotely (a situation where crew members are most likely to become confused). Tank suction handwheels are commonly painted a characteristic color, such as bright green. In addition, the tank number may be stencilled on deck next to the handwheel (1C, 3P, 5S, etc.).

In the same manner, crossovers and master valves are distinguished by the color of their handwheels (for example, masters painted yellow; crossovers, red and white). Stripping valves may also be color coded.

VLCC PIPING SYSTEMS

VLCC piping systems often resemble those used on smaller tankers. Pipelines, valves, pumps, and the tanks themselves are bigger, however, and the systems are more automated.

Some systems are unique to VLCCs. For example, a number of these big ships are fitted with a single pipeline, common to all tanks, which runs the length of the tank range. All of the pumps take suction through this line. Such an arrangement is possible because cargo separation is not a critical factor on crude carriers.

Free flow systems. On some VLCCs the main cargo piping can be bypassed. These ships make use of free flow systems, consisting of sliding gates provided at each tank bulkhead.

When these gates are opened (hydraulically), the usual stern trim of the ship causes oil to flow aft by gravity. Since the cargo pumps are located at the after end of the tank range, this arrangement allows efficient draining of the tanks with little or no need for stripping.

Inert gas systems. Explosion is an ever-present risk on tankers. On VLCCs—which employ high velocity, high volume tank washing systems—this danger is considered particularly great during tank cleaning operations. For this reason most new VLCCs are fitted with inert gas systems; these systems are designed to lower oxygen levels inside cargo tanks, thus inerting the atmosphere and making explosion impossible.

Flue gasses from the ship's boilers are used for this purpose. These gasses—mainly nitrogen and carbon dioxide—are cooled and filtered, then blown into the tanks with special fans. This is generally done through the vent piping (see next section) which is incorporated into the system.

The oyxgen content of inerted tanks normally remains at 5 percent or less—well below the amount needed to fuel an explosion. As an extra dividend, the rusting process inside the tanks is greatly inhibited by the use of inert gas.

See Chapter 8 for a further explanation of inert gas systems.

VENT SYSTEMS

When oil is loaded into an empty tank it displaces the air inside, causing a build-up of pressure. Similarly, when a full tank is discharged, oil leaving the tank pulls a vacuum behind it. In order to equalize these pressure differences, a vent line is needed.

On a typical handy-size tanker, vent lines run from the top of each tank to a vent header, or manifold, where several lines meet. From the header a single, larger line carries the vapors well up the mast, where they are vented to the atmosphere.

In this manner toxic and explosive fumes are allowed to dissipate at a safe distance from personnel and possible sources of ignition.

Vent headers are equipped with special valves called pressure-vacuum relief valves—PV valves for short (Fig. 28). PV valves are opened during cargo operations, thus leaving a free path through which air and vapors can flow.

After the tanks have been loaded, each PV valve is closed. This seals vapors inside the tanks and prevents loss of cargo by evaporation. In the closed position, PV valves are designed to lift whenever a significant pressure or vacuum develops inside the tank, as when cargo expands or contracts with temperature changes.

Vent headers are designed so

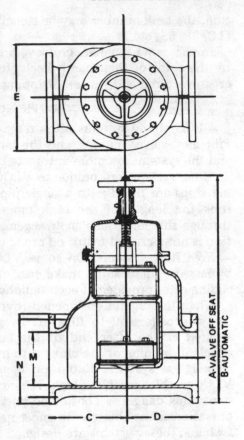

Fig. 28. Pressure-vacuum relief valve.
Hayward Manufacturing Company.

that one PV valve can serve several tanks. However, on some ships—most notably VLCCs—each tank may be equipped with its own vent line and PV valve.

Chapter 4

LOADING

Once, as a brand new third mate, I came within a hair's width of a disastrous spill. It happened, or nearly happened I should say, while I was standing a late-night loading watch on an old T2.

Fig. 29. Loading at an offshore terminal. Many terminals use single-point moorings (SPMs) like the one shown here. Gulf Oil Corporation.

The cargo, bunker fuel, was loading at a fairly slow rate; consequently I had decided to fill one tank at a time. While doing this I kept in mind one of the important rules of loading: *Always keep at least one tank open.*

The cargo must have somewhere to go, otherwise the pressure skyrockets as the shore pumps continue shoving oil down the closed-off pipeline. The result: a broken hose and a river of black oil flooding ship, dock, and surrounding water. I wanted to avoid that at all costs.

Everything went smoothly as we topped off 5 center, 6 center, and 7 center—always opening the next empty tank before closing the full one. One sailor opened as another one closed: a smooth, routine operation.

But then I made a mistake. As number 8 center topped off, I decided to shift to 2 center. Because the valve wheel for 2 center was on the foredeck, and therefore invisible behind the forward house, it was impossible to know for sure when the sailor there had opened it.

As 8 center came up to the mark, I signalled the foredeck with my flashlight. The sailor flashed in reply and I saw him disappear behind the forward house. It would take less than a minute for him to open 2 center.

I therefore felt safe, after waiting nearly a minute, when I told the sailor with me at 8 center to start closing.

Almost immediately I knew something had gone wrong. I heard a *clang!* as the man on the dock dropped a wrench. Unknown to me, his pressure gauge had skyrocketed past 200 pounds. He yelled, "*Hey! What's going on?*" and began running along the dock toward me.

Under my feet an ominous rattling vibrated from deep within the ship. Suddenly, I realized why—nothing was open. I had closed off against shore pressure!

I felt as though the blood had frozen in my veins. With shaking hands I grabbed the valve wheel and tried to reopen 8 center. The valve had jammed tight against the tremendous pressure; I couldn't budge it.

Trying not to panic, I signalled the sailor to help me. Frantically, with the adrenalin pulsing through our veins, the two of us strained at that valve wheel, tearing our fingers into a bloody mess.

We finally got it open, and the pressure dropped to a safe level. Quickly I ran to the foredeck and discovered the problem: somebody had lashed the valve wheel for number 2 center in the closed position. I found the sailor still struggling to untie the knot.

In the end no harm was done. We cut the lashing, opened 2 center, and closed 8 center in less than a minute. We had been lucky; only a miracle had prevented a broken hose and the resultant deluge of black oil.

Afterwards, as I stood there shaking, my hands covered with blood, I realized that I had learned an important lesson: a small mistake can, in an instant, turn a routine loading watch into a nightmare. That night I resolved to avoid such mistakes in the future.

BEFORE LOADING

Most tanker spills occur while loading; the loading operation should therefore command extra diligence from the ship's officers. Nearly all spills are preventable. Most are caused by human errors, with carelessness, impatience, and simple negligence leading the list.

The prevention of spills starts before the first barrel of oil enters the tanks. In fact, before any cargo operation, loading or discharging, the ship's officers perform a series of inspections which greatly reduce the chance of cargo contamination, spills, explosions, and fires.

Some companies use a checkoff list for this purpose. This is an excellent practice, especially since the accidental omission of even one item could cause a disaster. A new officer would be wise to make a list and use it religiously, even if his fellow officers do not.

Such a list should include the following items, each to be checked carefully before starting any cargo operation:

1. **Scupper plugs.** Make sure all deck scuppers have been plugged and, if necessary, cemented in place.

2. **Sea suctions.** While checking the pumproom, make sure the sea valves have been lashed in the closed position. They should never be secured with locks.

3. **Hose connections** should be checked for tightness, making sure a drip pan is in place under each.

4. **"Bravo" flag and red light** must be displayed prominently.

5. **Cargo system lineup.** At least two officers should check the lineup, paying particular attention to crossovers and drops. The appropriate drops must be open and, if loading two or more products, the crossovers separating these systems must be closed.

6. **Cargo tanks and tank valves.** Check that all tanks to be loaded are empty. Make sure each tank valve is closed, and remove the handwheel lashings from tanks to be loaded. Tanks already containing cargo should be lashed closed, in order to prevent accidental opening. In addition, it is a good idea to check void spaces, such as peak tanks and cofferdams, to make sure they are empty.

7. **PV valves** should be open on all tanks to be loaded.

8. **Pretransfer conference.** Find out the following from the terminal:

In what sequence will the various products load? What loading rate can be expected? How many shore pumps will be used? How much notice does the terminal need before the cargo finishes? What signal should be used for shutting down? Will there be a line displacement?

9. **Mark hoses with chalk.** It is a good idea to mark each hose with the name of the product being loaded (some officers even draw an arrow indicating direction of flow). In the event of a spill or broken hose, it would be disastrous to shut down the wrong product (it has happened!). The simple precaution of marking each hose can save you from this kind of blunder.

10. **Mark cargo status board.** This is most often a chalkboard with a plan of the cargo tanks superimposed on it (Fig. 30). Display this board in a prominent place, so that each watch stander can maintain a clear mental picture of all cargo activity. Mark the status of each tank with appropriate symbols indicating *open, closed, full,* or *empty.*

Fig. 30. The status of each tank is marked on a chalkboard. Chevron Shipping
Company.

11. **Declaration of Inspection.** This form lists certain inspections
which the law requires tankermen to perform prior to transfer of cargo
(Fig. 31). It must be signed by each watch officer and by the shore
operator.

Make sure a copy of this form is posted in a prominent place in the
ship's office; it is often the first thing coast guard officials look for
during periodic inspections.

When all inspections have been completed, the ship is ready to load.
Open the block valve at the manifold, plus the tank valve for each tank
to be loaded. Note these on the status board and give the dock the "go
ahead" to start loading.

START CARGO SLOWLY

Begin the transfer slowly, making sure there are no leaks at the hose
connections and that cargo is, in fact, entering the tanks. Do this by
checking the automatic tapes for movement, if your vessel is so
equipped.

At the same time make sure the float hasn't stuck to the bottom of
the tank—a common problem on ships carrying heavy, sticky fuel oils.
Roll the tape up and down several inches by using the hand clutch
fitted in the tapewell.

As oil flows into the tank, it is normal to hear the sound of air escaping around the ullage plug. This is a good sign that oil is, indeed, entering the tank and that all valves on the line are open.

REMOVING THE LIST

Some ships have a natural list, and this may cause problems when loading the wing tanks. Oil tends to gravitate toward the low side, causing a further tendency to list, which in turn causes more oil to gravitate, etc.

Therefore, one of the first steps when loading should be to remove the list. This is done by loading cargo in a wing tank on the high side of the ship until the list has been removed. Most experienced tankermen can tell "by eyeball" when their ship is straight, but it never hurts to check the clinometer, which is generally more precise.

STRESS

Stress is a vital consideration on tankers, even alongside the dock. Virtually all tankers tend to hog when empty, so it is important to avoid loading cargo in the extreme ends without placing some weight in the middle. The best procedure is to spread the load more or less uniformly through the tank range, thus equalizing stress and preventing a dangerous hog or sag condition during the loading operation.

On large ships stress must be checked at regular intervals—even hourly—while loading. This is most often done with a loading calculator or computer (see Chapter 6).

LOADING THE CENTERS

There are many methods of loading a tanker—almost as many methods as there are tankermen. So it is difficult to generalize or offer a single procedure to fit all circumstances. However, one generality holds true: all loading methods strive to fill the tanks without spilling oil. If your method accomplishes this, it is probably a good one.

Most tanker mates prefer to load the center tanks first, but this is not an immutable rule. A tanker can be loaded quite successfully by the opposite method—wing tanks first, then the centers. In most cases the exact method used is dictated by the chief mate.

Center tanks are considerably larger than wing tanks, and the cargo level rises more slowly. It follows that centers offer a greater margin of safety when topping off. During the final phase of loading, this margin of safety can be valuable, especially when the terminal is slow shutting down. It is therefore advisable to save at least one center tank for last.

LOADING THE WINGS

Early one morning several years ago, as I finished a long cargo watch, I learned something important about loading wing tanks.

AtlanticRichfieldCompany ◆
Marine Department

Declaration Of Inspection-
Prior To Bulk Cargo Transfer

Vessel		Date

Transfer facility		
	Port of	
	Location	

The following list refers to requirements set forth in detail in 33CFR 156.150 and 46 CFR 35.35-30, U. S. Coast Guard. (see reverse side).
The spaces adjacent to items on the list are provided to indicate that the detailed requirements have been met:

		Deliverer	Receiver
1.	Communication system/language fluency	(156.120 (m) (p))	
2.	Warning signs and red warning signals	(35.35 -30)	
3.	Vessels moorings	(156.120 (a))	
4.	Transfer system alignment	(156.120 (d))	
5.	Transfer system: unused components	(156.120 (e))	
6.	Transfer system; fixed piping	(156.120 (f))	
7.	Overboard discharges/sea suction valves	(156.120 (g))	
8.	Hoses or loading arms condition	(156.120 (h)) (156.170)	
9.	Hoses: length and support	(156.120 (b) (c))	

Fig. 31. Declaration of Inspection. A form similar to this one must be signed by each officer before he takes charge of the deck.
Atlantic Richfield Company.

10. Connections	(156.130)
11. Discharge containment system	(156.120 (j) (i))
12. Scuppers or drains	(156.120 (k))
13. Emergency shutdown	(156.120 (n))
14. Repair work authorization	(35.35 -30)
15. Boiler and galley fires safety	(35.35 -30)
16. Fires or open flames	(35.35 -30)
17. Lighting (sunset to sunrise)	(156.120 (t))
18. Safe smoking spaces	(35.35 -30)
19. Spill and emergency shutdown procedures	(156.120 (q))
20. Sufficient personnel	(156.120 (o) (s))
21. Transfer conference	(156.120 (q))
22. Agreement to begin transfer	(156.120 (r))

I do certify that I have personally inspected this facility or vessel with reference to the requirements set forth in Section 35.35-30 and that opposite each of them I have indicated that the regulations have been complied with.

Person in charge of Receiving Unit	Title	Time and date
Person in charge of Delivery Unit	Title	Time and date

Time completed

ARPE-4353 (4/75)

Fig. 31. (cont.)

49

S.S. Shasta Valley 　　　　LOADING ORDERS 　　　　Voyage # _21_

Product	API	T°	Gross	m	Net	BPT	Tons
Low Sulphur Fuel Oil	21.5	145	444,824	.9668	430,056	6.925	62,102
							Total　62,102

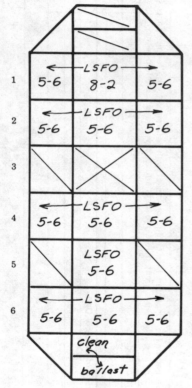

① Load to outages shown; #1 Center is final tank.

② Take gauges every 2 hours & figure rates. Also dial tonnages into loading calculator every 2 hours & watch the stress.

③ Take temp. of cargo at the riser every hour & note on blackboard.

④ There will be a 3000 barrel line displacement at the end of loading; inform the shore when #1 Center reaches an outage of _11'9"_ so they can shift tanks.

⑤ Shore will be using 2 pumps. Have them take one off the line if the pressure gets too high.

⑥ For any questions or problems, call me. Otherwise call me about one hr. before cargo finishes.

J. Thomas C/M

Draft:
F: 39-09
A: 42-07
M: 41-02

Fig. 32. The chief mate's loading orders.

As the center tanks topped off, my watch partners and I made a smooth changeover to the wings. Then, satisfied that things were running smoothly, I retired to the ship's office for a cup of coffee. I knew the sailors would keep the ship straight by pinching down valves on one side of the ship if cargo began to load too quickly on that side.

Because I was sleepy, I didn't notice the list immediately. But as I worked intently on a stack of paperwork, it seemed that I had to keep leaning farther and farther to starboard to sit upright. Suddenly I realized the ship had listed sharply to port—and she was tipping more all the time. I glanced out the porthole and gasped in disbelief—the deck had canted to a sickening, almost unreal, angle.

Apparently the sailors had become confused and pinched down the wrong set of valves. I rushed outside, yelling for them to open all starboard valves wide. At the same time I ran along the port side and closed those valves myself, stopping the flow of oil to the low side of the ship. In a few minutes, as quickly as she had listed, the ship straightened herself.

All tankermen must wrestle with this problem to a greater or lesser extent (hopefully lesser) each time they load the wing tanks. It is a job which requires constant scrutiny of the tape readings and careful adjustment of the tank valves.

The best advice is this: When one wing tank begins to load ahead of its counterpart, correct the situation immediately. This can be done by pinching down the heavy side or opening the light side, or both. After a few such adjustments the two sides should come up together or nearly so.

Wing tanks are small, relatively speaking. Depending on the ship, a wing tank may hold only 1/3 to 1/2 as much as a center tank. So use caution when loading wing tanks; they fill up quickly.

THE CHIEF MATE'S LOADING ORDERS

For the guidance of watch officers, the chief mate normally fills out a cargo plan with the following information: 1) products to be loaded in each tank; 2) final ullage for each tank; 3) API gravity and approximate temperature of each product; 4) total gross and net barrels of each product; 5) final draft and trim.

The mate posts this plan in a prominent place in the ship's office or cargo control room. In addition, he makes out a set of loading orders outlining the way in which he wants the cargo loaded (Fig. 32). Here he specifies loading sequence and any special instructions he may have, such as important valves to be opened, closed, or lashed. He also notes which tank or tanks should be loaded last.

Each officer is expected to study these orders carefully before taking charge of the deck. Should any doubt arise about the loading orders, it is always best to call the chief mate and ask him to clarify the situation.

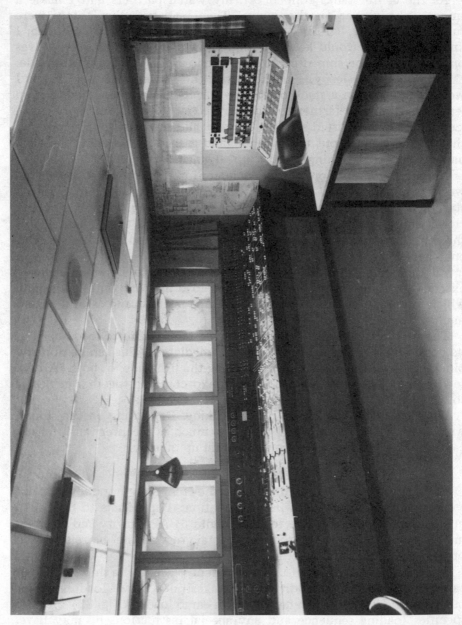

Fig. 33. Cargo control room. Kockums Automation AB.

THE LOADING WATCH

Therefore, the first step before taking over the loading watch is to study the chief mate's loading plan and orders. At this time you should also sign the Declaration of Inspection, if you have not already done so.

At the start of a loading watch, a good practice is to check every tank valve to make sure each is in the position indicated on the status board. Likewise you should check the ullage of every tank, not just the ones being loaded. This simple precaution has prevented many spills.

Oil moving into or out of a "closed" tank could indicate several potentially serious problems: 1) a valve which has been opened by mistake; 2) a broken reach rod; 3) a jammed valve; 4) a break in the below-deck piping.

If this happens, shut down until the source of the problem has been found and corrected.

Cargo control room. On automated tankers the cargo watch officer spends most of his time in the cargo control room (Fig. 33); from here he can monitor cargo levels and operate valves remotely. A typical control room contains the following: 1) cargo ullage indicators; 2) controls for valves and pumps; 3) cargo system pressure gauges; 4) tank atmosphere oxygen indicator (inert gas system); 5) loading calculator for figuring stress, draft, and trim; 6) communication equipment such as telephones and radios.

The cargo control room is normally located just below the bridge or in the upper area adjoining the pumproom. These locations give the watch officer a clear view of the main deck forward, through portholes or windows fitted for that purpose.

A light panel shows the status of all valves. For example, a red light might indicate closed; green, open.

The most sophisticated systems incorporate a computer terminal through which all important functions are controlled automatically. A program is fed into the computer at the start of loading (or discharging); it then performs all tasks without human assistance. The computer keeps track of tank ullages, opens and closes valves, and (when discharging) starts and stops pumps.

WHEN IN DOUBT, SHUT DOWN

Possibly the single most important thing for a new tankerman to learn is: *Never hesitate to shut down cargo operations.* Whenever in doubt, the first step should be to shut down. Do this *first;* then straighten out the problem. It is far better to lose a few minutes than risk a spill.

Shut down without hesitation in the following situations.

1. The pressure rises suddenly for no apparent reason.
2. You see oil in the water adjacent to the ship.

Fig. 34. Standing by to shift tanks. Seafarers International Union.

3. The hose fouls between ship and dock or begins to leak.

4. A valve or automatic tape jams.

5. You spot a fire on the dock or on another ship nearby.

6. The ship begins to drift away from the dock or the mooring lines become excessively slack.

7. A mooring line parts.

8. You smell smoke.

9. Another vessel approaches too closely.

10. Any other situation develops which could prove a hazard.

Anybody who wants to be a successful tankerman should engrave these words in his mind: *When in doubt, shut down.* Learn this, and you will keep the oil where it belongs—in the tanks.

GOOD PRACTICES

As mentioned previously, it is difficult to cover all possible situations when giving advice on loading. However, certain precautions and practices are common to all loading watches. Here are a few:

Watch the pressure. Pressure on the cargo system is usually low at the start of loading; in fact it may not register on the pressure gauges at all. As tanks fill up, pressure tends to rise slightly to perhaps 10-20 p.s.i. This should be kept within established limits for the vessel.

Cargo pressure while loading is proportional to the number of open tank valves. Close a valve, the pressure rises; open one, it falls. It is thus possible to decrease the flow of oil to a full or nearly full tank by opening one or more empty tanks.

This technique is particularly helpful when topping off, since it slows the loading rate to a safe limit. In fact it is often possible to stop the flow completely and gravitate cargo from a full tank to an empty one while still loading.

Never close off against shore pressure. Keep at least one tank open at all times or you will run the risk of a broken hose and a bad spill.

Watch the mooring lines. As a ship fills with cargo, she sinks lower in the water. At most docks this causes the mooring lines to become slack. In conjunction with a falling tide, this tendency may cause the ship to drift rapidly away from the dock, with resultant risk of broken hoses and loading arms.

For this reason, always keep a careful eye on mooring lines and tides. Don't hesitate to shut down, if necessary, while the sailors are tending lines.

Two men on deck. Practices vary, but it is generally a good idea to keep at least two men on deck, besides yourself, while loading. Most sailors are cooperative about this, as they should be—their job is to be on deck, not inside drinking coffee.

Closing valves. Make sure you and your watch use the proper method of closing valves. After closing, open one or two turns to flush the sediment from the valve seat; then close firmly, taking care not to jam.

Two-valve separation. On ships carrying refined products it is extremely important to keep the various systems separated, so that incompatible products cannot mix. Considering the time, effort, and expense involved in the refining process, it is not surprising that tanker companies want to avoid contamination.

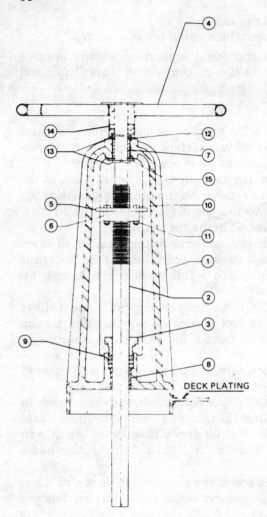

DECK PLATING

NO.	PART
1	BODY
2	STEM
3	GLAND
4	HANDWHEEL
5	INDICATOR PLATE
6	INDICATOR NUT
7	BUSHING
8	BUSHING
9	PACKING
10	HEX HEAD SCREW
11	LOCKNUT
12	THRUST WASHER
13	RETAINER
14	TENSION PIN
15	WASHER

Fig. 35. Valve operating stand on main deck. A metal reach rod connects the handwheel to a valve inside the tank. Each turn of the handwheel produces a corresponding turn on the valve. A threaded indicator, or *telltale*, registers the approximate number of turns the valve has been opened. Hayward Manufacturing Company.

Therefore, it is best to keep two closed valves between different cargoes whenever possible. This is an especially valuable procedure on old ships, where a single valve would be most liable to leak.

Ullages. Remember that ullages are measured from an above-deck datum, usually the top of the ullage hole. Thus a full tank will show an ullage of several feet.

Automatic tapes. Watch tapes for sticking or fouling, and keep them clean. Tapewells are fitted with squeegees to wipe the inside of the

Fig. 36. Proper alignment of loading arms is essential to prevent damage to connecting flanges. An Exxon Photo.

viewing window clear of condensation. Do not attempt to load a tank if the squeegee is worn or stuck. Have it repaired before opening the tank.

Hoses and loading arms. Check for proper alignment and support. Remember that hoses and loading arms form a fragile bond between ship and shore. They are easily broken.

Fig. 37. Sailors connect a cargo hose to the manifold. Hoses form a fragile bond between ship and shore; they must be properly tended and supported to prevent bursting. Seafarers International Union.

Heating coils. Certain cargoes (heavy fuel oils, for example) must be heated during the voyage to the discharge port. Steam heating coils are used for this purpose. As tanks top off, the chief mate may want the watch officer to turn on the heating coils. Check with him if in doubt.

Inert gas system. On ships fitted with inert gas systems, tanks are inerted before loading commences. As inert gas is displaced by cargo, it leaves the tanks through the vent system. Monitoring equipment in the cargo control room indicates the oxygen content in the tanks; in most cases this should remain below 5 percent. Each watch officer should keep a careful eye on the inert gas system while he is on duty.

Logbook entries. The logbook is an important document. Tanker companies rely on it as a vital source of information, and officers can be certain their entries receive careful scrutiny in the main office. In that regard be sure to make entries required by government and company regulations.

Include the following *times:* hoses connected/disconnected; start/finish of each product; any delays in the loading operation and their cause.

Smoking. Make sure crew members smoke in authorized areas only. Be particularly wary of visitors and workers from ashore who may "light up" without thinking.

Vessel security has become an important consideration in recent years. Be careful not to allow unauthorized individuals aboard, and stay alert for suspicious activity on (or under) the water adjacent to the ship.

OFFSHORE MOORINGS

With the steady increase in the size of tankers, a need has developed for deepwater terminals to accommodate them. Many of these new terminals are offshore moorings, where a ship ties up to one or more buoys in deep water well off the land. (When necessary, VLCCs can also be lightered to smaller vessels; see Fig. 38.)

Cargo is loaded/discharged through a special hose attached to a submerged pipeline. The pipeline runs along the sea bottom to a terminal or tank farm on the adjacent shore.

There are basically two types of offshore moorings: multi-point and single-point.

Multi-point moorings have been in use for years and are common off the coast of the United States. A ship moors by dropping both anchors —one at a time and carefully spotted—and backing into a nest of five or more buoys (Fig. 39). A mooring line is run from the ship to each buoy. The ship is thus held in position by the balanced tension of mooring lines and anchor chains.

Cargo is loaded through a submerged hose which descends to a pipeline on the seabed. Prior to loading, the hose is hauled aboard by means of a cable attached to a hose buoy in the mooring.

Single-point moorings, or SPMs, are a more recent development. Figures 29 and 40 illustrate typical SPMs. The ship makes her bow fast to the buoy, after which a floating hose is brought aboard and fastened to the manifold. Swivels allow the ship to pivot freely around the buoy with changes in wind and tide.

Loading at an offshore mooring. Operating procedures at an offshore mooring differ from those at a regular dock. One of the most important differences is communication; because the terminal is located far from the ship—perhaps a mile or more—radios must be used.

On nonautomated tankers, where the mate on watch spends most of his time on deck, portable radios are used. These can be carried from tank to tank. Each officer must learn to operate the radio before taking

Fig. 38. Lightering operation at sea. A 209,000-d.w.t. VLCC discharges
part of her cargo to a smaller vessel (71,000 d.w.t.). For the VLCC, this
is basically a discharging operation; for the smaller vessel, a loading
operation. Lightering is often used when VLCCs must enter shallow
ports which cannot accept them fully loaded. A Shell Photo.

over the deck. Automated vessels are normally equipped with a permanent radio installation in the cargo control room. (In addition, portable
UHF radios are often used for onboard communication between mate
and sailors.)

The radio should be tested at regular intervals during each watch.
Messages to the terminal should be spoken slowly and clearly. After

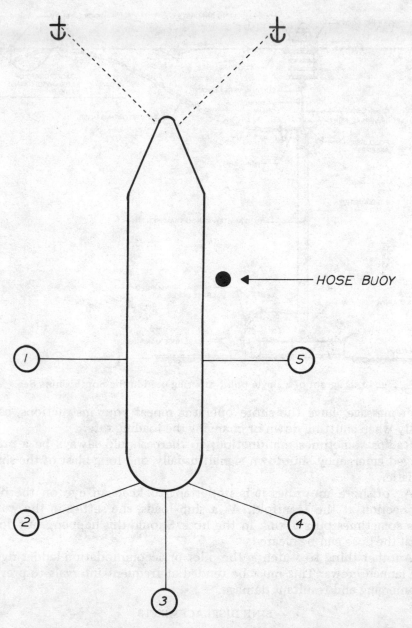

Fig. 39. Diagram of a multi-point offshore mooring. The ship's anchors are carefully positioned and dropped, one at a time, prior to backing into a nest of buoys. A mooring line is run to each buoy. The ship is thus held in position by the balanced tension of mooring lines and anchor chains. A cable attached to the hose buoy runs to a submarine hose, which is hauled up from the seabed with the ship's hose boom.

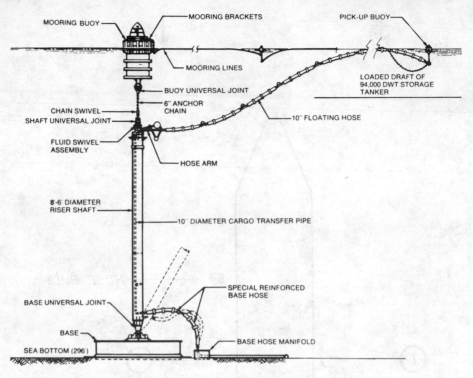

Fig. 40. Diagram of a single-point mooring used in the South China Sea.

each message, have the shore operator repeat your instructions, especially when shutting down or changing the loading rate.

Radios sometimes malfunction, so there should always be a prearranged emergency shutdown signal: usually one long blast of the ship's whistle.

At offshore moorings it is important to keep an eye on the hose connection at the manifold. As a ship loads, she settles in the water; this sometimes puts a kink in the hose. Should this happen, shut down until the hose can be cleared.

Another thing to watch is the pilot or accommodation ladder rigged for launch crews. This must be tended at frequent intervals to prevent submerging and resultant damage.

LINE DISPLACEMENTS

During the final phase of loading, the terminal may want to fill their pipeline with another product, possibly in preparation for the next ship due at the dock. This is called a *line displacement*.

For example, if the pipeline from shore tank to ship holds 3,000 barrels, the terminal will ask to be notified when the ship's gauges indicate 3,000 barrels to go. At this point they will stop their pumps

Fig. 41. Portable radios are often used for communicating with the terminal, and for onboard communication between mate and sailors. Chevron Shipping Company.

and switch tanks (or they may do a "flying switch"). By the time loading is completed, 3,000 barrels of new product will displace the old product and push it aboard the ship.

Generally speaking, the two products involved must be similar (two grades of gasoline, for example) so that a few barrels of mixing, which is inevitable, won't matter.

On the other hand, lines containing heavy crude or fuel oil are often displaced with a light product, such as diesel. This is particularly true at offshore moorings where submerged hoses would otherwise become clogged by the heavier products.

Gauging a line displacement. Let's assume the terminal has asked you to gauge a 3,000-barrel line displacement. You will have no trouble doing this as long as you load the last 3,000 barrels in one tank (the chief mate has probably specified which one).

Let's assume this tank is number 1 center, with a final ullage of 8′ 2″. With the calibration tables you determine that this ullage corresponds to 44,447 gross barrels (you need not be concerned with net barrels when figuring line displacements).

Since you want to stop the cargo 3,000 barrels short, you subtract this amount from the final figure for the tank: 44,447 - 3,000 = 41,447.

Referring to the calibration tables once again, you select the ullage which most nearly corresponds to 41,447 barrels: 11' 9" (see Fig. 42). Armed with this information, you watch the tape at number 1 center until it reads 11' 9" (trim corrections can be ignored). At this point you signal the dock, indicating 3,000 barrels to go.

After the terminal switches tanks, you load the remaining cargo, bringing number 1 center to the final ullage of 8' 2". By the time you give the final signal to shut down, the shore line will be full of new product.

S.S. SHASTA VALLEY
Cargo Tank #1 Center

ullage	barrels	ullage	barrels
8' 00"	44586	10' 00"	42914
01"	44517	01"	42843
02"	44447	02"	42774
03"	44377	03"	42705
04"	44308	04"	42635
05"	44238	05"	42565
06"	44168	06"	42495
07"	44099	07"	42426
08"	44029	08"	42356
09"	43959	09"	42286
10"	43889	10"	42217
11"	43820	11"	42147
9' 00"	43750	11' 00"	42077
01"	43680	01"	42008
02"	43611	02"	41938
03"	43541	03"	41868
04"	43471	04"	41798
05"	43402	05"	41729
06"	43332	06"	41659
07"	43262	07"	41589
08"	43192	08"	41520
09"	43123	09"	41450
10"	43053	10"	41380
11"	42983	11"	41311

Fig. 42. Gauging a 3,000-barrel line displacement. Loading is stopped at 11' 9", or 2,997 barrels short of the final amount. (A small discrepancy of three barrels is caused by rounding off to the nearest inch.)

LOADING TO FINAL DRAFT

Unlike some types of merchant ships, tankers—most notably crude carriers—frequently load to the maximum draft permitted by law. In other words, many petroleum cargoes are heavy enough to load a ship "down to her marks."

Classification societies (such as the American Bureau of Shipping, Lloyd's Register of Shipping, and Norske Veritas) place draft marks on newly built vessels. The use of these marks is required by law as set forth in the Load Line Regulations (see Chapter 6).

When the chief mate draws up his cargo plan, he calculates the exact number of barrels to be loaded in order to submerge the ship to her marks. He must, however, work with information which may not be completely accurate. For example, the values for API or temperature may be slightly off, or the chief engineer may have more bunker fuel in his tanks than estimated.

With these potential inaccuracies in mind, it would not be surprising for the final draft to differ by several inches from the calculated value. Such a discrepancy causes one of two things: an overloaded ship, which is illegal, or an underloaded ship, which is less profitable for the company.

To avoid these pitfalls it is necessary to monitor the draft from the dock during the final minutes of loading, signalling the terminal to shut down just as the ship submerges to her marks. As a rule, the chief mate does this while one of the other officers keeps track of the ship's tanks. (It is usually impossible to take an accurate draft at offshore moorings; the common practice is to rely on the calculated values.)

Before loading to draft, a sample of the water alongside the ship must be taken. All tankers carry a simple hydrometer for measuring specific gravity; this value tells how much dock water allowance to use. The sample should be taken within the final hour of loading, since water densities often change with the tide. (See Chapter 6 for a discussion of fresh and dock water allowances.)

TRIMMING THE SHIP

Trim is often a vital consideration on tankers. For example, the master may want his ship flat for crossing a shallow bar. Then again, anticipating a large burnoff from after bunker tanks on a long voyage, he may want several feet of stern trim.

In most cases the chief mate's calculations for trim are accurate. However, he must anticipate some variation, just as he did in loading to draft. It may therefore be necessary to adjust the final trim, in one of several ways: 1) by loading more cargo forward or aft; 2) by shifting cargo when loading has finished; 3) by shifting bunkers; 4) by ballasting.

The latter method would not be used on a fully loaded ship, but it could be used in the case of a partial load. In most situations the second method of shifting cargo is the easiest. This can often be done by *gravitation*, a technique which uses the natural tendency of oil to flow from a full tank to an empty or slack tank.

For example, if the ship has too much stern trim, simply open one or more full tanks in the after end of the ship, plus one or more empty or slack tanks in the midship or forward sections. Gravity will cause cargo to flow to the forward tanks. When the desired trim is reached, close the valves.

This technique is more apt to be used on a single-product ship where cargo separation is not a problem. On a multi-product ship, the problem of shifting cargo may require a more complex lineup plus the use of one or more cargo pumps.

AFTER LOADING

When the last tank has been topped off and secured, the vessel is made ready for sea. Hoses and loading arms are drained and disconnected. Cargo tanks are ullaged, and temperatures are taken. PV valves are closed, and ullage plugs are pinned shut.

The vessel is now ready to proceed to the next port and a different phase of the transfer operation—the discharge.

Chapter 5

DISCHARGING

The typical tankerman regards a discharging watch as a pleasant interlude—a time to relax, a respite from the tension of loading watches. After all, with the cargo moving out rather than in, it couldn't spill. The pumpman watches the pumps and generally runs the show. Why not kick back and relax?

Fig. 43. Crew members prepare to hook up mammoth loading arms prior to discharging a VLCC. Nearly 200,000 tons of oil will flow through these pipes before the ship is empty. A Shell Photo.

Unfortunately, this attitude is as dangerous as it is common. A new officer should avoid it at all costs.

Let your fellow officers slack off during discharging watches, if they must, but you should stay alert. Discharging a tanker can be just as risky as loading one, and it requires the same meticulous care as other operations.

A friend of mine learned this lesson the hard way. He and I were shipmates on a tanker several years ago; he was third mate, I was second. One day, while we were discharging a cargo of heavy crude at a refinery near San Francisco, a serious spill occurred. My friend was on watch, and he ultimately shouldered the responsibility for the mishap.

I had just returned from a trip ashore. When I reached the top of the gangway, I was shocked to find the deck gang cleaning up a large spill. A puddle of crude oil had spread across the after deck and over the fish plates. The water surrounding the ship was covered with a greasy slick.

The captain, chief mate, and refinery executives stood on deck, forming an angry circle around the luckless third mate. Together they demanded: "What happened?"

"I don't know," he told them. "We weren't even discharging yet. It just doesn't seem possible."

What *did* happen?

The watch had started uneventfully enough. Because of a problem in the refinery, discharging had not begun. The terminal informed the third mate that they would not be ready to receive cargo for at least an hour. So, with nothing better to do, my friend retired to the officers' lounge for a cup of coffee. Taking the cue, both sailors also left the deck.

In the meantime, the pumpman decided to open some tanks in preparation for the discharge. He opened several center tanks and, to save time later, he also opened the block valve at the riser. Then he, too, went inside for some coffee.

The deck was therefore deserted when oil began to bubble out of number 8 center.

Let's take a look at how this happened. The shore tank was located on a hill above the ship. The valves to this tank were open, as were the valves on the dock. The oil thus travelled by gravity from the shore tank to the ship, where it made its way through the open riser valve and into the tanks by way of a leaky check valve in one of the pumps. (Check valves are designed to prevent this kind of backflow but, like any mechanical device, they sometimes malfunction.)

The resultant spill would not have been serious had it been detected immediately. Unfortunately, almost 15 minutes slipped by before action was taken. During that 15 minutes oil slowly puddled on deck, overflowed the fish plates, and spilled into the harbor.

Any one of four men—third mate, pumpman, two sailors—could have prevented this spill. But, like too many tankermen before them, they fell victim to a false sense of security while discharging. They let their guard down—and suffered the consequences.

PRETRANSFER CHECKOFF

Devote as much care and effort to discharging as you would to loading and you will avoid serious problems. This effort starts with the pretransfer checkoff. As when loading, it pays to use a checkoff list (see Chapter 4).

Make sure scuppers are plugged, sea suctions closed and lashed, hoses securely bolted and supported, loading arms properly aligned, and warning signals displayed.

Check the lineup carefully. Drop valves must be closed; otherwise cargo could recirculate and cause a spill. In addition, check each tank valve and remove the handwheel lashings from tanks to be discharged. Mark the hoses and status board carefully, and sign the Declaration of Inspection.

Check with the terminal regarding cargo sequence, size of shore line, line displacements, and emergency shutdown signals. Will there be a booster pump on the shore line? If so, make sure they start it in the right direction (pumping oil *away* from the ship).

THE PUMPMAN

The coast guard requires a special examination and certification before allowing an individual to sail as pumpman. As his title implies, the pumpman operates and maintains the cargo pumps. He goes into action anytime the pumps are used: while discharging, ballasting, tank cleaning, or whenever cargo is transferred between tanks.

His job is physically exhausting, and the hours are long. For this reason many ships carry two pumpmen.

More than any other member of the crew, the pumpman must know the lineup intimately. He is potentially an excellent teacher. A new officer would do well to follow him through the cargo lineup, and stay by him during ballasting and tank cleaning.

But a word of warning: No man is infallible, including the best pumpman. In the end, the officer on watch wields the authority and bears the final responsibility.

If you suspect the pumpman is doing something unwise or illegal (like pumping bilge slops into the harbor at midnight), don't be afraid to speak up. He probably doesn't know the pollution regulations as well as you do. If a conflict should develop, call the chief mate and let him resolve it.

TYPES OF CARGO PUMPS

Although the pumpman operates and maintains the pumps, it is important for the ship's officers to understand this equipment thoroughly. The following types of pumps are likely to be encountered on tankers: 1) reciprocating; 2) centrifugal; 3) rotary (such as gear or screw pumps); 4) jet (such as eductors); 5) propeller.

Of these, the first two—reciprocating and centrifugal—are by far the most common. We will therefore confine our discussion to these two principal types.

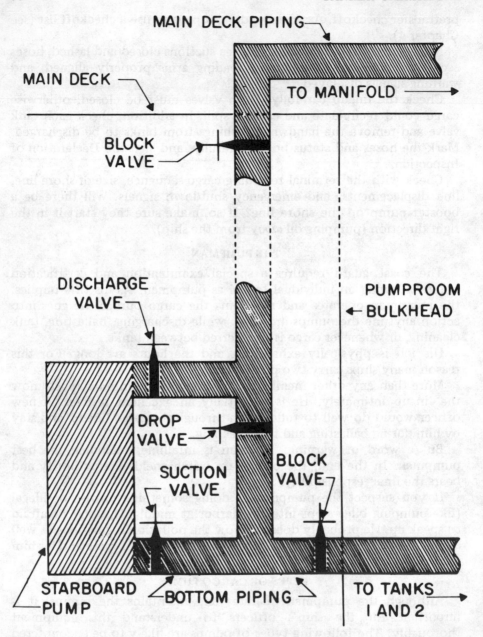

Fig. 44. Simplified diagram, side view, of the starboard pump, associated valves, and piping, as might be fitted in a three-pump pumproom. Bill Finhandler.

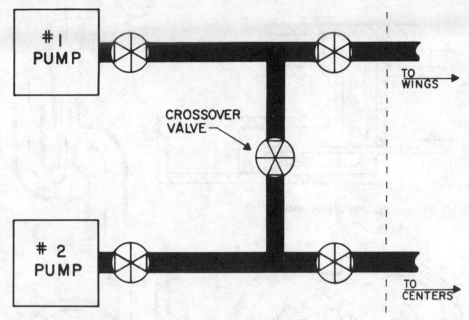

Fig. 45. Simplified diagram, top view, of a two-pump pumproom (bottom piping only). By opening or closing the crossover valve, pumps can be isolated or made "common." Thus, number 1 pump could be used in the center tanks or number 2 could be used in the wings. Similarly, both pumps could be made common and used to pump out a combination of wings and centers simultaneously. *Note:* A typical pumproom contains stripping pumps, bilge pump, ballast pump, and associated piping, valves, etc.—none of which are shown here. Bill Finhandler.

Reciprocating pumps. Until World War II, reciprocating pumps served faithfully as the primary means of discharging cargo. The subsequent development of efficient centrifugal pumps has largely eclipsed their use, but reciprocating pumps remain in service on many modern ships, mainly as stripping pumps.

A basic reciprocating pump consists of a piston—usually powered by steam—which slides back and forth in a cylinder. On the intake stroke the movement of the piston creates a vacuum, thus drawing oil into the cylinder through the intake valve. On the discharge stroke the piston forces oil through the discharge valve, creating a pressure on the discharge side of the pump.

Early reciprocating pumps were of simple design, but eventually the more sophisticated duplex pumps came into use (Fig. 47). These are essentially two pumps in one, designed so the intake stroke of one synchronizes with the discharge stroke of the other. The result is greater capacity and smoother operation.

Reciprocating pumps are sometimes called *positive displacement pumps.* Unlike centrifugal pumps they need not be fed by gravity, and

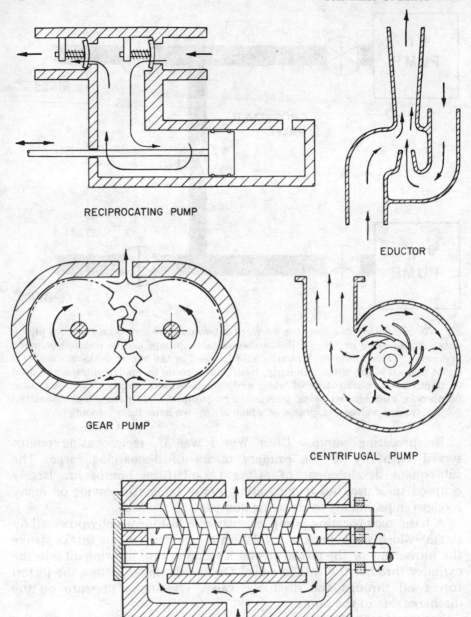

RECIPROCATING PUMP

EDUCTOR

GEAR PUMP

CENTRIFUGAL PUMP

SCREW PUMP

Fig. 46. Common types of pumps. U.S. Coast Guard.

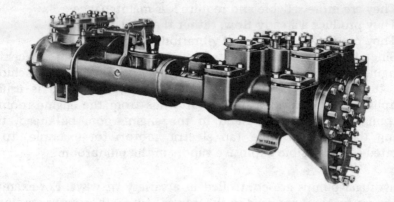

Fig. 47. Reciprocating pump. Worthington Corporation.

can pump a tank to the bottom until dry. This is an important advantage.

Some older ships employ reciprocating pumps exclusively—thus eliminating the need for separate stripping pumps and much additional piping for a stripping system.

But reciprocating pumps have one serious drawback—they are slow. It would take days or even weeks to discharge a modern supertanker with reciprocating pumps; time which translates into thousands of dollars in lost revenue. Today's tanker therefore requires a faster means of discharging cargo.

Centrifugal pumps fill this need. These are continuous-flow, gravity-fed pumps, consisting of one or more spinning impellers. These impellers draw oil through a central inlet and hurl it outward by centrifugal force. This action creates a vacuum on the inlet side and pressure on the discharge side of the pump.

Centrifugal pumps cannot function without a continuous gravity-flow of cargo. For this reason they are generally located in an after pumproom, thus using the normal stern trim to drain cargo more efficiently.

From their position at the bottom of the pumproom, centrifugal pumps can draw cargo to within one or two feet of the bottom of each tank. The residue is then removed through a separate stripping system, usually employing reciprocating or some other type of positive displacement pumps.

Centrifugal pumps are superior to reciprocating pumps in several important ways:

1. They pump more cargo in less time.
2. They are smaller, more compact, and easier to install.
3. They are less expensive.

4. They are more reliable and require less maintenance.

5. They produce a steady flow, rather than pulsating.

6. They produce less noise and vibration.

7. Since they are usually located in an after pumproom adjacent to the engine room, they can adapt to various power sources, including steam turbines, electric motors, and diesel engines. This is usually accomplished as follows: a drive shaft runs from the engine room to each pump via a gastight gland in the engine-room bulkhead, thus allowing the power source (an electric motor, for example) to be segregated from possible explosive vapors in the pumproom.

Centrifugal pumps are controlled in a variety of ways. For example, when steam turbines are used as the power source, the pumps are started and stopped by operating the tur-bine steam valves, either remotely from the cargo control room or manually at the turbine itself.

On older ships the pumps are often controlled from the engine room; it is therefore necessary to call the engineers to start or stop a pump. In an emergency, however, the pumps can be shut down quick-ly by operating special switches provided for this purpose. These are commonly located near the pumproom.

When using centrifugal pumps always be careful to switch tanks in ample time to avoid losing suc-tion. Generally speaking, tanks can be taken to within 1½ or 2

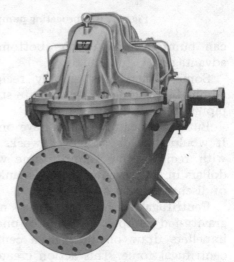

Fig. 48. Centrifugal pump. Worthington Corporation.

feet of the bottom on medium size tankers; then the stripping pump must take over.

If allowed to run dry, a centrifugal pump will suffer serious damage in a matter of minutes; it might even explode. With experience, your ears will become sensitive to the high-pitched whine of a pump about to lose suction.

Some newer types of centrifugal pumps are self-priming. In some cases air exhausters are fitted to help prevent pumps from losing suction. Another method is to provide a continuous flow of oil to the impellers—as with a stripping pump lined up to take suction from the discharge side of the main pumps.

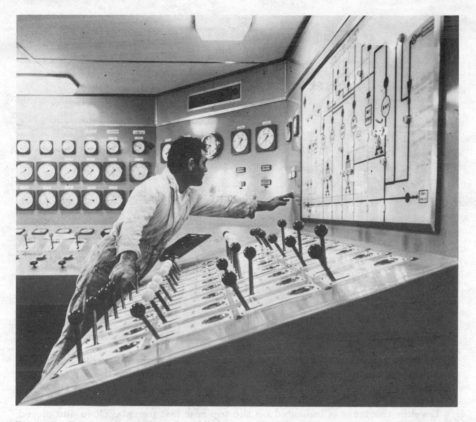

Fig. 49. Cargo control room. Discharging is virtually a one-man operation on board this 207,000-d.w.t. VLCC. A Shell Photo.

These devices make it possible to take the tanks much lower with the main centrifugal pumps, and when used carefully they virtually eliminate the need for stripping.

Deepwell pumps are centrifugal pumps of special design, used mainly on ships carrying a great diversity of refined products.

Each pump is permanently installed above an individual cargo tank. The impeller is located at the end of a long vertical shaft extending to the bottom of the tank. The shaft is enclosed in a discharge pipe which carries oil from the impeller to the above-deck piping.

This arrangement takes advantage of the speed and efficiency of a centrifugal pump while minimizing the disadvantages. Because the impeller operates so close to the bottom of the tank, it can discharge nearly all cargo before losing suction. Stripping is usually unnecessary.

Cargo separation is therefore greatly enhanced in that only one pump is used for each tank so fitted.

Fig. 50. Cargo control console for a 90,000-d.w.t. tanker. Seventy-five valves required for control of cargo oil and ballast water systems on the San Clemente Class Tankers being built by National Steel and Shipbuilding in San Diego are controlled hydraulically and electrically from this central console.

Level in the tanks is indicated on the top row instruments. Open and closed valve positions are shown by the lights on the ship's mimic diagram. The ballast, cargo and stripping pump speeds and pressures are controlled from the controls below the mimic area.

Ballast and cargo valves are actuated by pushbutton controls on the mimic area of the console. Manufactured by Paul-Munroe Hydraulics, Pico Rivera, California.

PRIMING THE PUMPS

Both reciprocating and centrifugal pumps occasionally become air-bound and fail to pick up suction on a tank. In such instances it is necessary to prime the pump from a full tank or, in some cases, to bleed air from the discharge side of the pump by opening a vent cock.

Centrifugal pumps will not operate unless filled with oil, so it is sometimes necessary to prime them before beginning the discharge. To do this, open a full tank on the same line as the pump, then open the vent cock on the pump. You will hear the sound of air escaping from the vent cock. When a steady stream of oil replaces the air, the pump is full (primed) and ready for use. (As we learned earlier, some centrifugal pumps are fitted with air exhausters which make venting unnecessary.)

Reciprocating pumps. It is rarely necessary to bleed air from a reciprocating pump when starting on a full tank. A few strokes will flood the cylinders with oil and force air out the discharge line, thus eliminating the need to open the vent cock.

Therefore, when a reciprocating pump does lose suction, it can almost always prime itself from a full tank. Priming in this manner eliminates the need for a special trip into the pumproom to open the vent cock.

When stripping the last few barrels from a tank, the pump tends to draw in air from the surface of the oil. To avoid this—and resultant loss of suction—reduce pump speed and pinch down the tank valve. This will lower the gate of the valve below the level of the oil, thus excluding air from the valve aperture.

A helpful trick is to listen at the ullage hole. A gurgling noise from inside the tank indicates the pump is sucking air. When you hear this noise, pinch down the valve until the gurgling stops. When it resumes, pinch down some more. In this manner you will keep the edge of the valve gate below the surface of the oil.

There are times, however, when loss of suction is unavoidable. When this situation arises —and no full tank is available for a prime—slow the pump and bleed air by opening the vent cock. In most cases the pump will regain suction immediately.

Reciprocating pumps, like centrifugal pumps, make a characteristic sound when losing suction. Each pump is a little different, but they all tend to race when sucking air. When you hear a reciprocating pump losing suction, quickly reduce the speed of the pump and begin pinching down the tank valve.

Controls for reciprocating pumps are, for the most part, located at the top or just outside the pumproom. These consist of a handwheel for each pump fitted to a reach rod. The reach rod descends to the bottom of the pumproom and

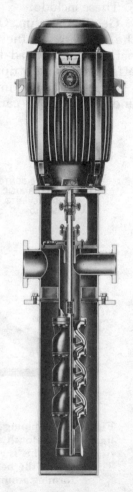

Fig. 51. Deepwell pump. Worthington Corp.

attaches to the steam valve on the pump. When the valve is opened, the pump starts; closed, it stops. (Learn the location of control wheels for all pumps; they are not always marked.)

Reciprocating pumps are designed to operate efficiently within a given range of strokes per minute, usually up to about 30. They tend to lose suction when allowed to run fast.

DISCHARGING PROCEDURE

There are as many ways to discharge a tanker as there are to load one, so no step-by-step instructions can be given. However, certain principles apply to all discharging watches.

These include:

Get the bow up. On ships with an after pumproom, it is best to start the discharge in the forward tanks. This lifts the bow and provides a better suction head to the pumps. In addition, the tanks drain more effectively while stripping.

Strip residual oil into a single tank. Stripping pumps are not powerful enough to move cargo against the high pressure of large centrifugal

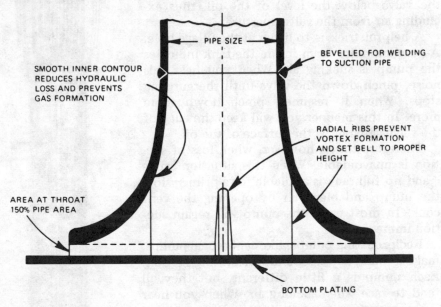

PIPE SIZE

SMOOTH INNER CONTOUR
REDUCES HYDRAULIC
LOSS AND PREVENTS
GAS FORMATION

BEVELLED FOR WELDING
TO SUCTION PIPE

RADIAL RIBS PREVENT
VORTEX FORMATION
AND SET BELL TO PROPER
HEIGHT

AREA AT THROAT
150% PIPE AREA

BOTTOM PLATING

Fig. 52. Tank piping flares into a suction bellmouth at the end of each branch line. The bellmouth allows pumps to draw suction very close to the bottom of the tank. This is vital during stripping, when air tends to leak into the line. The design of the bellmouth also helps to prevent eddies, or whirlpools, from forming around the intake. Hayward Manufacturing Company.

pumps. Therefore, instead of trying to strip ashore against the main line pressure, it is standard practice to accumulate stripped oil in one tank on board the ship.

Thus accumulated, most of it can be discharged with the main cargo pumps. The last few barrels can be stripped ashore after the main pumps shut down.

More often than not, the aftermost center tank (which adjoins the pumproom) is used for this purpose. A special filling line runs from the stripping system into the tank.

This tank is normally full at the start of discharging. It is therefore necessary to pump it down part way before stripping into it. Later in the discharge as the strippers pump residues into the tank, causing the level to rise, it may be necessary to pump out additional cargo with the main pumps.

Always watch this tank carefully. If left unattended it could easily overflow and cause a spill when least expected.

Check pumproom frequently. Make regular inspections of the pumproom, checking for leaks and excessive vapor accumulation. (This is also a good idea while loading. I once sailed with an officer who failed to do so and found out later that a broken line had filled the

Fig. 53. Shifting tanks. The smaller handwheel operates the stripping valve. Chevron Shipping Company.

pumproom with gasoline.) Check the pumps for smooth operation, and make sure the drive-shaft seals, where the pump drive shafts enter the engine room, are not overheating.

A gassy pumproom can kill you. Before entering, always make sure the ventilation system is operating. Have a man stand by topside while you're below, in case you should be overcome by vapors (pumproom gassing is perhaps the most common serious accident on tankers). This simple precaution has saved numerous lives.

Two-valve separation. If possible, try to keep at least two closed valves between systems containing unlike cargoes.

Watch the pressure. While discharging, pressure on the cargo system is normally much higher than it is while loading. For example, a pressure of 120 p.s.i. at the riser might be considered typical (as opposed to perhaps 15-20 p.s.i. while loading).

Pressure should be monitored carefully, because it tends to change, sometimes appreciably, as tanks are topped off in the terminal. Be prepared to change pump speed or place additional or fewer pumps on the line.

Chief mate's discharging orders. The chief mate generally writes a set of discharging orders detailing sequence, pumps to use, maximum pressure, key valves to open or close, and anything else he thinks important. Study these orders carefully before taking charge of the deck.

Logbook entries. Pay the same scrupulous attention to logbook entries as you would while loading.

When in doubt, shut down. Learn the location of the emergency shut-down switches, or similar controls, for each pump—and don't be afraid to use them.

Automatic tapes. After discharging a heavy or sticky product such as bunker fuel, the automatic tape floats tend to stick to the tank bottoms. If you suspect this may happen, have the pumpman or one of the sailors roll up the tapes. This is easily accomplished with the hand clutch on each tapewell. A sliding forked bar is fitted on the tapewell to hold floats in the upper position.

Heating coils. To avoid damage to the heating coils, turn off the steam to individual tanks well before each is empty.

Mooring lines. At most docks, mooring lines tend to tighten as the ship rises. A rapidly rising tide combined with a fast discharge could easily part one or more lines. (At places such as Anchorage, Alaska, this sort of thing is almost routine. I served on one ship which parted the same mooring wire three times in one 24-hour period in Anchorage.)

Watch the mooring lines carefully and, if necessary, shut down while the sailors tend them.

Stress. Plan the discharge carefully to avoid excessive stresses on the hull. When starting the discharge most of the cargo will come from the forward tanks, but don't overdo it. A certain amount should be pumped from the aft and midship sections as well, in order to equalize the stress.

Booster pumps. When a shore tank is located at a great distance from the ship, or on top of a hill, an additional pump or pumps are frequently put into use along the shore line. This helps to reduce pressure and increase the rate of discharge. In general, the terminal waits until the ship has started discharging before putting booster pumps on the line.

Whenever a booster pump is to be used, be sure to start the discharge slowly. Watch the pressure; it should drop sharply within a few minutes, indicating the booster pump is on the line. It is now safe to increase the discharging rate by speeding up the ship's pumps or placing more pumps in service.

If, however, the pressure *rises* sharply when the booster pump is brought on the line, immediately shut down the ship's pumps and close the manifold valves. The terminal has lined up the booster pump in the wrong direction (a not unheard-of occurrence) and is pumping oil *toward* the ship.

List. Control of list is essential during the discharge, especially while stripping. When a ship is allowed to list excessively, residual oil pools on the low side of the tanks, where it may not drain properly to the bellmouths. As a result, and unacceptable amount of oil is left in the tanks.

To avoid such pitfalls, list must be carefully controlled. This is done mainly by keeping each pair of wing tanks even, a task which requires careful observation and adjustment.

However, this in itself may not be enough to keep the ship from listing. For example, a temporary list is often induced when the engineers shift bunkers or water from one side of the ship to another. Then again, some tankers are built with a natural list (caused by a slight imbalance in the arrangement of engine room machinery).

In such situations, you must compensate by counterbalancing a single pair of wing tanks. For example, you might choose number 5 wings to eliminate a port list. This would be accomplished as follows:

Pump out number 5 port until the ship straightens herself; then close number 5 wings, port and starboard. If a new list should develop, use these two wing tanks to straighten the ship by pumping cargo from the low side. Save number 5 wings to be discharged last, so that positive list control can be maintained throughout the discharge.

Inert gas systems. As cargo is discharged, the inert gas system (assuming your ship has one) will be operating. Most systems are designed to maintain a slight pressure of inert gas inside the tanks, to prevent air being drawn in. This pressure also speeds the discharge to some extent (at least in theory) by providing a better head to the pumps.

During your watch, monitor the oxygen content inside the tanks (normally shown on an indicator inside the cargo control room). Make sure it does not exceed permissible limits for your ship. (Anything below 10 percent is generally considered safe, but most tanker companies require the oxygen content to be kept well below this—often at 5 percent or less.)

SPILLS

Spills are less common while discharging than while loading, but they still occur. Several situations can lead to a spill:

Broken hose or loading arm. This is a too-common occurrence, caused by defective equipment, improper support, or excessive pressure.

Improper lineup. An open drop valve on a discharge line will cause cargo to recirculate to the tanks—where it could overflow.

Defective check valve. Centrifugal pumps are fitted with check valves to prevent oil from gravitating through the pumps and into the tanks. These check valves are not infallible and they sometimes stick.

If the manifold valves are opened several minutes before starting the pumps, back pressure from the shore line could force cargo through the pump and into the tanks. A slight back-flow to a full tank could easily cause a spill.

With this in mind, *always leave the manifold block valves closed until ready to start discharging.*

Gravitation. When a tanker is trimmed by the stern, cargo tends to gravitate toward the after tanks. Thus, if full tanks forward and aft are opened several minutes before starting the pumps, cargo will have time to flow aft and could cause a spill.

Therefore, *leave tank valves closed until ready to start discharging.*

Overflow of stripping fill tank. Keep a careful watch on the tank used to accumulate stripping residues. Never allow it to fill above a safe level.

LINE DISPLACEMENTS

On light-oil product carriers, the first phase of the discharge sometimes occurs while still docked at the loading port.

This is the pump and line flush. A small amount of oil is discharged with each pump (into the terminal slop line), thus flushing the discharge piping and assuring that each pump and its system are full of the correct product. If the pumps are to discharge more than one product, care should be taken to flush with the first product in the discharging sequence.

When a ship arrives at her port of discharge, the terminal sometimes asks for an initial line displacement. This procedure clears the shore line of other products. In order to facilitate gauging, it is best to restrict the discharge to a single tank during the line displacement. (Chapter 4 describes the procedure for gauging a line displacement.)

Line displacements are also common at the end of the discharge, particularly on black-oil ships. Many heavy fuel oils and some crudes solidify to the consistency of shoe polish when allowed to cool; they can clog pipelines unless flushed clear.

A ship loaded with such a cargo will therefore oncarry a tank of diesel or other light stock for the final line displacement. After all cargo has been discharged and stripped, the light stock is flushed through the ship's pumps and pipelines and is then pumped ashore.

This clears the heavy oil from all lines, both on board and in the terminal.

Chapter 6

PLANNING THE LOAD

How many tankers have been lost as a result of improper cargo planning? Nobody knows. But this much is clear: Tankers show an alarming tendency to break in half during heavy weather. An improperly distributed load greatly augments this tendency.

Cargo planning is essential on tankers just as it is on freighters. But where transverse stability is a constant worry on freighters, it is rarely a problem on tankers. Tankers are inherently stable, and values for GM are almost never calculated.

However, another important factor comes into play—*stress.* Loads must be carefully spread through the tank range to minimize the shear and bending stresses on the hull. A tanker's steel hull will bend with remarkable elasticity, but if bent too far, it will break.

Stress is not the only consideration. In addition, the ship must be loaded to a proper draft and trim. Unlike cargoes must be assigned to separate tanks and, if necessary, to separate systems.

THE VOYAGE ORDERS

The chief mate normally decides how these problems are to be dealt with, and it is his responsibility to draw up the final loading plan. The decision is not his alone, however. The ship's owner or charterer specifies (by radio) how much cargo to load and, frequently, which tanks to put it in. Experienced cargo planners in the company's main office work out each load in advance.

Voyage orders are usually wired to the ship in code for the purpose of speed and economy. After decoding, a typical set of orders might read as follows:

S.S. Shasta Valley, voyage 21. Proceed Barber's Point, Hawaii. July 1 load approximately 62,000 tons low sulphur fuel oil. API 21.5, temperature 145. Tanks 1 across, 2 across, 4 across, 5 center, 6 across. Oncarry 1300 tons clean ballast in afterpeak and after clean ballast tanks. Bunkers 1400 tons. Water 210 tons. Discharge entire cargo Long Beach, California. Tentative orders voyage 22: load Drift River, Alaska; discharge Los Angeles.

These orders should never be followed blindly, because cargo planners are human and make mistakes. The chief mate must check their figures; he bears the final responsibility for the load.

At this point we should note the role of junior officers in cargo planning. Although the chief mate shoulders most of the responsibility, it is important for the second and third mates to develop a thorough understanding of the procedures involved.

Fig. 54. Heavy weather generates tremendous bending stresses on a tanker's hull.

As a junior officer, you should make every effort to learn about cargo planning. First of all, this knowledge will help you to perform your own duties more efficiently. For example: stress, draft, and trim must be checked at frequent intervals—even hourly—during loading and discharging on many ships. This task must be performed by the mate on watch, usually a second or third mate.

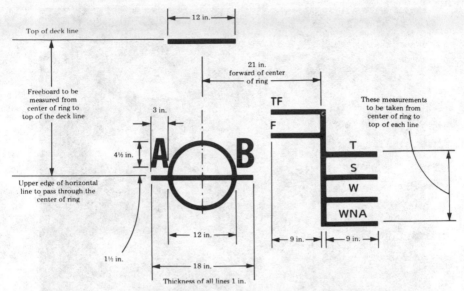

The center of the ring is to be placed on each side of the vessel at the middle of the length as defined in the Load Line Regulations. The ring and lines are to be permanently marked, as by center punch, chisel cut or bead of weld.

A B	American Bureau of Shipping
T F	Tropical Fresh Water Allowance
F	Fresh Water Allowance
T	Load Line in Tropical Zones
S	Summer Load Line
W	Winter Load Line
W N A	Winter North Atlantic Load Line

Fig. 55. Load line markings for oceangoing vessels. These are placed amidships on both sides of the hull. The American Bureau of Shipping is authorized to assign load lines to vessels registered in the United States and other countries. Requests for the assignment of load lines are to be made on forms which will be furnished by one of the offices of the Bureau. American Bureau of Shipping.

In addition, a thorough knowledge of cargo planning is essential for your eventual promotion to chief mate and, finally, to master.

LOAD LINES AND ZONE LIMITATIONS

Early in the history of seafaring, sailors and shipowners recognized the importance of cargo planning, which included strict limits on the total weight carried each voyage. These early seafarers realized that an overloaded ship, although carrying more potential revenue, rode dangerously low in the water. She thus became vulnerable to the attacks of the sea.

As long ago as 2500 B.C., Greek vessels were required to undergo loading inspections before venturing into the Mediterranean. During the

Fig. 56. ABS inspectors check a vessel's load line markings. American
Bureau of Shipping.

Middle Ages, the city-state of Venice enforced similar laws on her
vessels—each marked her load line with a cross painted on the hull.

The Scandinavians were equally careful; in the fierce gales of the
North Sea their lives depended on it. A Swedish law written in 1288

declares: "If goods are loaded above the load line, the owner must either put the excess goods ashore or pay a fine."

But it was not until the 19th century that a universal standard for load lines began to emerge. Samuel Plimsoll, a member of the British Parliament and an ardent crusader for seamen's rights, pushed for the adoption of stringent load line regulations. Against stiff opposition, he succeeded.

The first of these laws passed from Parliament in 1876, and by the time of Mr. Plimsoll's death in 1898 virtually every maritime nation had followed Great Britain's example. Today we still refer to a vessel's load line as her "Plimsoll mark" in remembrance of Samuel Plimsoll.

Standards for today's ships are set by the *International Convention on Load Lines, 1966*. These international standards, drawn up by the maritime nations of the world, have been incorporated into Federal laws, which are enforced by the U.S. Coast Guard. The coast guard also publishes a set of *Load Line Regulations (CG-176)* for use by merchant vessels.

When a ship is new, the appropriate load line markings are etched permanently on her hull (both sides, amidships) by an authorized classification society. In the United States this task is performed by the American Bureau of Shipping (ABS).

Each mark corresponds to a given *displacement*, or total tons of water displaced by the vessel. This tonnage is exactly equal to the weight of the loaded ship.

Marks are provided for Tropical, Summer, Winter, and Winter North Atlantic zones for both fresh and salt water. (Because salt water is more buoyant than fresh, allowance is made for the extra sinkage in fresh water—the *fresh water allowance*.)

This system permits vessels to load more deeply in regions of predominantly fair weather and during seasons when good weather can be expected (see Chart, Fig. 57). For example, a tanker loading in Valdez, Alaska (Winter Seasonal Zone) on December 1st would load to her winter marks. In contrast, a ship loading in Rio de Janeiro, Brazil (Tropical Zone) would be allowed to load to her tropical marks.

Zone allowance. However, a ship which has loaded to her tropical marks in Rio de Janeiro is unable to venture north or south into the Summer Zone without violating the law.

She is governed not only by the zone in which she loads, but also by those through which she must sail. If her course takes her through the Summer Zone, *she must not be loaded below her summer marks at any time while inside that zone.*

The trick is to load maximum tonnage allowable while making sure the ship will not be overloaded as she sails from one zone to another. Allowance can be made for the burnoff of bunker fuel and consumption of fresh water while steaming toward the *controlling zone* (that is, the strictest zone through which the vessel must sail).

Thus the *zone allowance* represents the extra tonnage a vessel may load beyond that permitted by the controlling zone. This figure is easily calculated on the basis of bunker fuel burnoff and water consumption.

For example:

A tanker loads at a terminal within the Tropical Zone. She will enter the Summer Zone approximately nine days after departing the loading port, and the approximate burnoff at sea speed is 50 tons/day. Water consumption is 10 tons/day. How many tons may she load beyond that allowed by her summer load line?

By simple arithmetic:

zone allowance = 9 days x 60 tons/day
= 540 tons

Note that a ship sailing in the other direction (that is, from Summer Zone to Tropical Zone) would not require this calculation; she would already be in the controlling zone.

IMPORTANT TERMS

In order to provide a clear understanding of cargo planning on tankers, a few terms should be explained at the outset:

Deadweight. This is the total weight of cargo, plus crew, stores, water, fuel, and ballast on board at a given time.

Displacement. When a ship floats freely in the water, the weight of water displaced by her hull is exactly equal to the weight of the ship. Thus the term *displacement* is used to denote a vessel's weight, in long tons of 2,240 pounds apiece, at a given draft.

Deadweight scale. Figure 58 shows the deadweight scale of a typical tanker. This is a handy device for determining the mean draft corresponding to a given deadweight or displacement. Important hydrostatic values, such as tons per inch immersion (TPI), are also listed for various drafts.

Light ship. This is the displacement, or weight in long tons, of a vessel minus cargo, crew, stores, fuel, water, and ballast; in plain words, the weight of the empty ship.

Tons per inch immersion (TPI). Change in draft is proportional to the amount of weight loaded or discharged. The number of tons required to submerge a vessel one inch amidships, or TPI, varies with the draft. Values for TPI can be found on the deadweight scale or in tables drawn up from this data.

This information is valuable when computing changes in mean draft caused by weights loaded or discharged. The following formula is used:

$$\frac{\text{weight loaded (or discharged)}}{\text{TPI}} = \text{change in mean draft}$$

Let's illustrate with an example:

A tanker's mean draft is 25′ 00″. At this draft the value for TPI is 150 tons/inch. What will be her new draft after loading 900 tons?

Using the formula:

$$\frac{900 \text{ tons}}{150 \text{ tons/inch}} = 6'' \text{ increase in draft}$$

$$\begin{array}{r} 25'\ 00'' \\ +\quad 6'' \\ \hline 25'\ 06'' \end{array} = \text{new mean draft}$$

Trim is simply the difference between forward and after drafts, expressed either in feet or inches.

Tipping center, or center of floatation, could be described as a hinge about which a vessel rotates longitudinally. This hinge is not fixed in a single position but slides forward and aft with changes in draft and trim.

Longitudinal center of buoyancy (LCB) is the center of volume of the underwater part of a vessel's hull, and is the point through which all upward forces of buoyancy are assumed to act.

Longitudinal center of gravity (LCG) is the counterpart of LCB, or the point through which all *downward* forces of a vessel's weight are assumed to act. More precisely, LCG represents a vessel's center of mass (as viewed longitudinally, or from the side).

As we will discuss later in this chapter, LCB and LCG act together to form a trimming lever, or arm, which trims a vessel about her tipping center. The position of LCB and LCG relative to each other determines the amount of the final trim and whether it will be by the head or by the stern (Fig. 59).

Values for LCB are found in tables or hydrostatic curves supplied by the naval architect. LCG is calculated by a method we will discuss shortly. When both values are known, trim can be computed by simple arithmetic.

Trimming moment. When a weight is loaded or discharged at a given distance forward or aft of the tipping center, a *trimming moment* is created. Likewise, a moment is created when a weight already on board is shifted forward or aft. Moments are expressed in foot-tons and are computed by the formula:

trimming moment = weight (tons) x distance (feet)

Moment to change trim one inch (MT1) is used in conjunction with trimming moments to determine change in trim. MT1 varies with the draft; values are found on the deadweight scale or tables derived from it.

Let's illustrate the use of MT1 with an example:

A tanker has a draft of 25′ 00″ forward and aft (vessel on even keel). MT1 at this draft is 1,000 foot-tons. Suppose 100 tons is moved aft 100 feet; what are the new drafts?

Fig. 58. Deadweight scale for a 70,000-d.w.t. tanker. Bethlehem Steel Corporation.

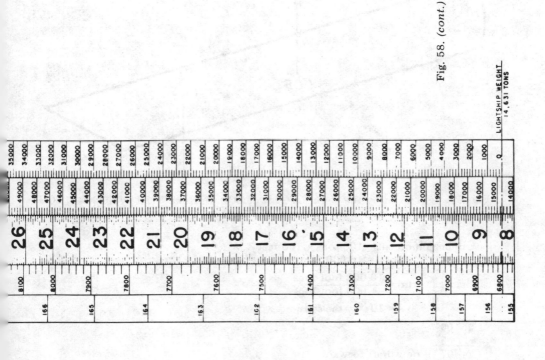

Fig. 58. (cont.)

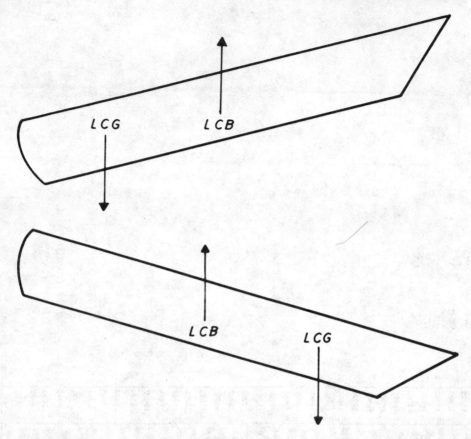

Fig. 59. *Top:* Trim by the stern; LCG aft of LCB. *Bottom:* Trim by the head; LCG forward of LCB.

trimming moment = 100 tons x 100 feet
                = 10,000 foot-tons

change in trim = $\dfrac{10{,}000 \text{ foot-tons}}{1{,}000 \text{ foot-tons}}$

                = 10″ by the stern

$\dfrac{\begin{array}{r} 25'\ 00'' \\ -\quad\ 5'' \end{array}}{24'\ 07''}$ = new draft forward

$\dfrac{\begin{array}{r} 25'\ 00'' \\ +\quad\ 5'' \end{array}}{25'\ 05''}$ = new draft aft

Note that the new drafts are determined by applying *half* the change in trim to forward and after drafts respectively. Because the weight has moved aft in this case, we add 5 inches to the after draft and subtract the same amount from the forward draft.

When a weight is loaded or discharged, we encounter a slightly different problem. The first step is to determine the new mean draft produced by the change in displacement. Change in trim can then be computed and applied to the new mean draft to determine the new drafts forward and aft.

Let's go back to the ship used in the preceding example. Once again, let's give her an initial draft of 25′ 00″ forward and aft, plus an MT1 of 1,000 foot-tons. TPI at this draft is 50 tons/inch.

Suppose 100 tons is loaded 100 feet aft of the tipping center; what are the new drafts?

$$\text{increase in mean draft} = \frac{100 \text{ tons}}{50 \text{ tons/inch}} = 2''$$

25′ 00″
+   2″
25′ 02″ = new mean draft

trimming moment = 100 tons x 100 feet
                = 10,000 foot-tons

$$\text{change in trim} = \frac{10,000 \text{ foot-tons}}{1,000 \text{ foot-tons}}$$
$$= 10'' \text{ by the stern}$$

25′ 02″
-      5″
24′ 09″ = new draft forward

25′ 02″
+   5″
25′ 07″ = new draft aft

Fresh and dock water allowances. As we noted earlier, fresh water is less buoyant than salt water; a vessel therefore requires less tonnage to submerge her applicable load line in fresh water. The load line regulations allow for this fact, and each ship is assigned a *fresh water allowance* equal to the number of inches her mean draft will change when moving from fresh to salt water in a fully loaded condition.

Merchant ships rarely sail in completely salt-free water, but it is not uncommon to enter a harbor formed by a mixture of salt and fresh water (as at the mouth of a river). Here the term *dock water allowance* comes into play.

Dock water allowance is the number of inches a ship may load below her marks in water of a given density, or specific gravity. A water sample is taken during the last hour of loading, and the specific gravity is measured with a simple hydrometer.

The specific gravity of fresh water is 1.000; of salt water, 1.025. Dock water often falls somewhere in between. Thus the dock water allowance is found by a simple proportion. This is best shown by example:

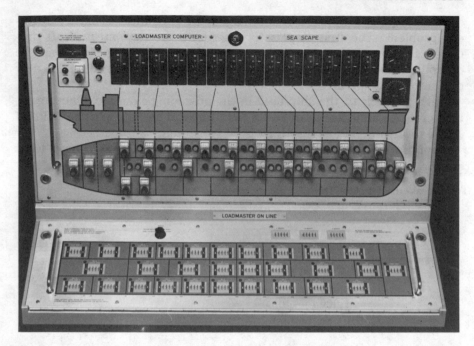

Fig. 60. The Kockums *Loadmaster* Computer can be used to precalculate cargo distribution and can also be connected to the automated gauging system. In the latter mode it provides a continuous automatic read-out of stress, trim, and draft. Kockums Automation AB.

On a ship with a fresh water allowance of 10 inches, a water sample is taken and the specific gravity is found to be 1.010. What is the dock water allowance?

Table 7

DOCK WATER ALLOWANCES

(fresh water allowance = 10″)

Specific Gravity	Allowance
1.000 (fresh)	10″
1.005	8″
1.010	6″
1.015	4″
1.020	2″
1.025 (salt)	0″

We know this: at specific gravity 1.000, the allowance would be 10 inches; at 1.025, zero inches. Our value of 1.010 falls 10/25 of the way between 10 inches and zero or, going the other way, 15/25 of the way between zero and 10 inches.

Thus:

dock water allowance $= \dfrac{15}{25} \times 10'' = 6.0''$

Many people find this calculation confusing and, for this reason, a table of dock water allowances such as the one shown in Table 7 is normally used.

LOADING PLAN AND CALCULATIONS

Earlier in this chapter we used a set of voyage orders for the *Shasta Valley* as an example. Let's look over the chief mate's shoulder as he calculates the load and fills out the loading plan for voyage 21 (see Fig. 61).

His first problem is to find out which load line must be used. Barber's Point lies within the Seasonal Tropical Zone (tropical marks in July). Long Beach, on the other hand, is in the Summer Zone. The ship must therefore load to the summer displacement, plus a small amount for zone allowance.

At summer marks the *Shasta Valley* displaces 79,863 tons. The mate knows from experience that she will require about 43 hours, or 1.79 days, to reach the Summer Zone at sea speed. He also knows that fuel and water consumption at sea speed equals about 100 tons per day. He therefore calculates zone allowance as follows:

zone allowance = 1.79 days x 100 tons/day
                   = 179 tons

He adds this tonnage to the summer displacement to ascertain the maximum displacement to which the *Shasta Valley* may load at Barber's Point.

79,863   (summer displacement)
+   179   (zone allowance)
80,042 = loaded displacement

Referring once again to the deadweight scale, or tables, the mate finds that a displacement of 80,042 tons corresponds to a mean salt water draft of 41' 02''. This will be the *Shasta Valley*'s loaded draft at Barber's Point.

How many tons of cargo must be loaded to reach this draft and displacement? From the voyage orders, the mate knows this figure should be somewhere around 62,000 tons, but he must come up with the exact tonnage. His first step is to figure total noncargo tonnage, as follows:

Light Ship	14,877
Fuel	1,400
Water	210
Crew and Stores	118
Ballast	1,335
Total	17,940 = noncargo tonnage

S.S. SHASTA VALLEY Voyage # _21_ Date: _7-1-77_

Product	API	T°	Gross	m	Net	BPT	Tons
Low Sulphur Fuel Oil	21.5	145	444,824	.9668	430,056	6.925	62,102
						Total	62,102

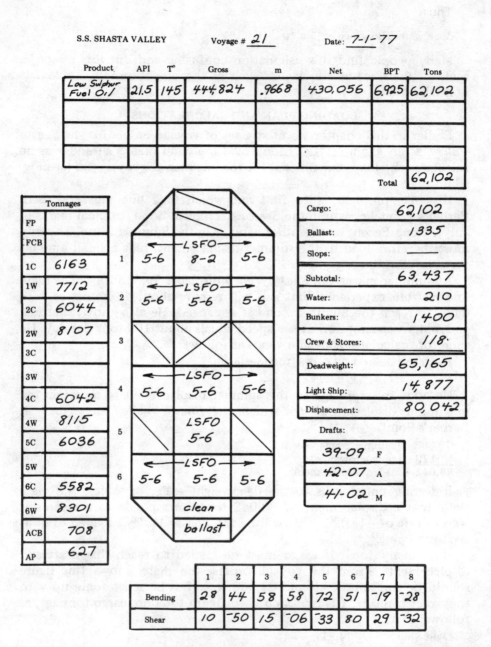

Tonnages	
FP	
FCB	
1C	6163
1W	7712
2C	6044
2W	8107
3C	
3W	
4C	6042
4W	8115
5C	6036
5W	
6C	5582
6W	8301
ACB	708
AP	627

Cargo:	62,102
Ballast:	1335
Slops:	—
Subtotal:	63,437
Water:	210
Bunkers:	1400
Crew & Stores:	118
Deadweight:	65,165
Light Ship:	14,877
Displacement:	80,042

Drafts:

39-09	F
42-07	A
41-02	M

	1	2	3	4	5	6	7	8
Bending	28	44	58	58	72	51	‾19	‾28
Shear	10	‾50	15	‾06	‾33	80	29	‾32

Fig. 61. Loading plan.

96

Since cargo must make up the remaining tonnage, the mate simply substracts noncargo tonnage from displacement to determine cargo tonnage to load:

        80,042   (loaded displacement)
       -17,940   (noncargo tonnage)
        62,102 = tons of cargo to load

Using the values given for API and temperature, the mate can now figure total net and gross barrels (for a review of this procedure, see Chapter 2). This accomplished, he must distribute the gross barrels of cargo throughout the tanks in such a manner as to produce an acceptable stress and trim.

To simplify this task, the mate searches through old cargo plans in the hope of finding a similar load to use as a model. Luckily, he finds one in which the same cargo, at approximately the same tonnage, was loaded. He discovers that number 3 across and number 5 wings were left empty (3 and 5 wings are clean ballast tanks), number 1 center slack, and the remaining tanks full.

Using this distribution as a guide, the mate fills out a tentative plan (Fig. 61). How about stress and trim? The *Shasta Valley* is equipped with a loading calculator (see Figs. 60, 62, and 63) and these values are easily determined.

The mate enters the tonnages for each tank into the calculator; he then reads off values for forward and after drafts, plus stress, directly from the face of the machine. Draft: 39' 09" forward, 42' 07" aft, 41' 02" mean. The mean draft is correct, since it corresponds to the desired displacement. The trim, 34" is also satisfactory.

The calculator indicates shear and bending stress numerals for each of eight points along the hull. None of these may exceed 100 (the maximum stress numeral permitted on the *Shasta Valley*).

The mate checks each of the points and finds them all within acceptable limits. The plan can therefore be used as it stands.

FORMS FOR CALCULATING STRESS AND TRIM

Many ships (old ones, most notably) are not equipped with loading calculators like the one used on the *Shasta Valley*. Stress and trim must therefore be worked out mathematically.

A form such as the one shown in Fig. 64 is normally used, along with a hand calculator, and the procedure is a relatively simple one.

Trim. As we discussed earlier, the longitudinal center of buoyancy (LCB) and longitudinal center of gravity (LCG) act together to trim a ship (Fig. 59). When LCG falls aft of LCB, trim is by the stern; when LCG is forward of LCB, trim is by the head.

In order to calculate the final trim, we must first locate LCB and LCG. LCB is a hydrostatic value which changes with draft and trim; it

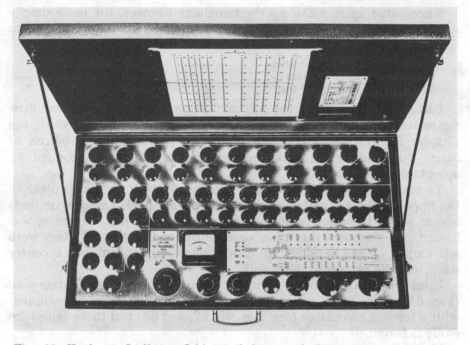

Fig. 62. Kockums *Lodicator* L4A, used for precalculating cargo distribution. Kockums Automation AB.

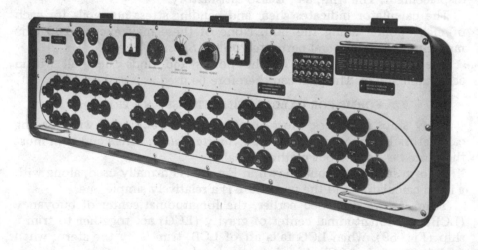

Fig. 63. The Sperry-Sintep Loading Calculator. Sperry Marine Systems.

can be found in tables or curves provided by the naval architect (see Table 8). The location of LCB is given in feet forward or aft of the centerline (or other fixed part of the vessel, such as the forward perpendicular).

Table 8

S.S. HILLYER BROWN
(17,000 d.w.t.)

Displacement	LCB	MT1	Draft
6,000	257.55	1542	9-04½
6,500	257.5	1561	10-01
7,000	257.42	1576	10-09
7,500	257.36	1591	11-05
8,000	257.3	1610	12-01
8,500	257.25	1621	12-09
9,000	257.2	1632	13-04
9,500	257.09	1650	14-01
10,000	257.0	1660	14-09
10,500	256.89	1672	15-04½
11,000	256.8	1685	16-00½
11,500	256.7	1694	16-08½
12,000	256.6	1711	17-04½
12,500	256.49	1721	18-00
13,000	256.38	1737	18-08½
13,500	256.23	1749	19-04½
14,000	256.1	1761	20-01½
14,500	255.93	1780	20-09
15,000	255.81	1791	21-05
15,500	255.7	1808	22-00½
16,000	255.55	1822	22-08½
16,500	255.33	1840	23-04½
17,000	255.18	1857	24-00
17,500	255.01	1873	24-07½
18,000	254.89	1890	25-02
18,500	254.65	1910	25-11
19,000	254.5	1928	26-05½
19,500	254.3	1945	27-02
20,000	254.09	1965	27-09½
20,500	253.92	1983	28-06
21,000	253.73	2000	29-00½
21,500	253.48	2020	29-08½
22,000	253.32	2040	30-04
22,500	253.05	2063	30-11
23,000	252.87	2082	31-07
23,500	252.65	2102	32-02
24,000	252.43	2127	32-10

LCG is another matter. In order to make this calculation, LCGs for each tank (taken from tables) are multiplied by their tonnages to determine a moment for each. The same calculation is made for light

TANKER STRESS AND TRIM DETERMINATION C-96

FOR USE WITH STRESS AND TRIM TABLES

| OUTAGES | | GROSS | TEMP | TANK | PRODUCT | NET | °API | LONG | STRESS NUMERALS | | MOMENT |
FEET	INCHES	BARRELS	°F			BARRELS	GRAV	TONS	HOG	SAG	
XXXXXXXX				TOTALS FOR CARGO			XXX				

Fig. 64. Form for calculating stress and trim. Chevron Shipping Company.

	OTHER THAN CARGO	XXXXXXXXX	XXX	XXXXXXXXXXX	XXXXXXXXXXX	XXXXXXXXXXX	XXXXXXXXXXXXXXXXXX
BUNKERS							
FRESH WATER							
MISCELLANEOUS	CREW AND STORES						
LIGHT SHIP	SUB-TOTALS						
	LIGHT SHIP						
	TOTALS						
STRESS	SUBTRACT STRESS DEADWEIGHT CORRECTION (.0____ TIMES SUB-TOTAL)						XXXXXXXXXXXXXXXXXX
	RESULTANT STRESS NUMERALS (MUST NOT EXCEED 100, EXCEPT 12 FOR T-1's)						XXXXXXXXXXXXXXXXXX
TRIM	TOTAL LONG TONS TIMES LONGITUDINAL CENTER OF BUOYANCY						
	REPEAT "TOTAL" SHOWN ABOVE IN "MOMENT" COLUMN AND MAKE SUBTRACTION						
	RESULTANT TRIM MOMENT (IF INVERTED SUBTRACTION, TRIM IS BY THE HEAD)						
	DIVIDE RESULTANT TRIM MOMENT BY MOMENT OF TRIM PER INCH AT DRAFT ______ = ______ INCHES OF TRIM BY STERN HEAD						
DRAFT	TOTAL LONG TONS (DISPLACEMENT) EQUALS SALT WATER MEAN DRAFT OF FEET INCHES						
	COMPUTED DRAFT: FORWARD; AFT; MEAN.						
	OBSERVED DRAFT: FORWARD; AFT; MEAN. DENSITY ALLOWANCE INCHES						

VESSEL	VOYAGE NO.	LOADING PORT	DATE	DESTINATION

C-96 (5M-CD-10-65)
PRINTED IN U.S.A.

Fig. 64. *(cont.)*

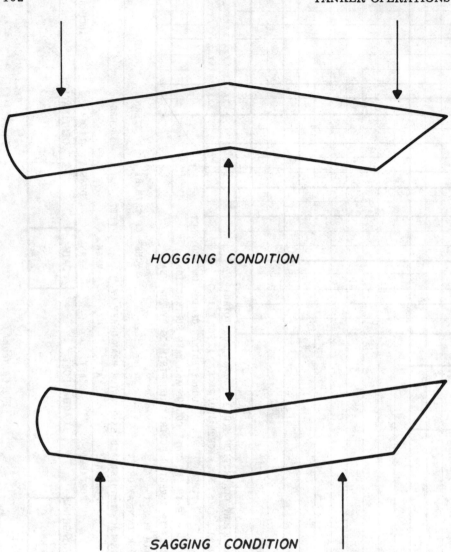

HOGGING CONDITION

SAGGING CONDITION

Fig. 65. *Top:* Hogging condition is caused by too much weight in the extreme ends, too little amidships to counter the buoyant force of water beneath the hull. *Bottom:* Sagging condition is caused by too much weight amidships.

ship, fuel oil, fresh water, etc. The sum of all moments is divided by displacement to determine the distance of LCG forward or aft of the centerline (or whichever reference point is used).

The *trim arm* is the longitudinal distance between LCG and LCB. It is multiplied by the ship's displacement to find the total trimming moment. This total moment can then be divided by MT1 to find the trim.

Simply stated:

trim arm = longitudinal distance between LCG and LCB

$$\text{trim (inches)} = \frac{\text{displacement x trim arm}}{\text{MT1}}$$

By another method, the total trimming moment is determined by adding up the moments for the various tanks, light ship, fuel oil, fresh water, etc. This total is subtracted from the product of LCB times displacement. The resultant trimming moment is, as before, divided by MT1 to determine trim. Therefore, by the second method:

(LCB x displacement) — (sum of moments)
= total trimming moment

$$\text{trim} = \frac{\text{total trimming moment}}{\text{MT1}}$$

Stress can be divided into several constituents. *Shear stresses* occur when two forces act in opposite directions parallel to one another, as at a bulkhead between an empty tank (pushed up by buoyancy) and a full tank (pushed down by the weight of cargo).

Hogging occurs when a ship loads too heavily at the ends, causing the middle to bend upward. *Sagging* occurs when a ship loads too heavily in the middle, causing it to bend downward (Fig. 65).

When a ship puts to sea, such stresses are greatly augmented by the action of the swells, which can create a dangerous condition in a poorly loaded tanker.

Stress can be computed mathematically when no loading calculator is available. A form similar to the one used for trim is generally used. As a rule, stresses are resolved into a *stress numeral* for each tank or point along the hull. None of these numerals may exceed the maximum allowed for the vessel.

LOADING TO FINAL DRAFT

As we discussed in Chapter 4, the loading plan serves basically as a guide or approximation of final tank ullages, draft, and trim. These rarely turn out exactly as expected.

For example, an inaccurate estimate of API or temperature would cause an error in the calculation of gross barrels. As a result, more (or less) gross barrels would have to be loaded in order to reach the desired draft.

For this reason, the final loading to draft should be done by observation from the dock whenever practicable.

Chapter 7

BALLASTING

Fifteen centuries ago, a tribe from northern Germany—the Saxons—invaded England. The Saxons were a seafaring people; they brought a colorful vocabulary of nautical terms with them to England. The word *barlast* (literally, "bare load") referred to heavy weights (or cargoes carried because of their heaviness) which, when stowed in the hold of an empty ship, greatly increased stability. This is the probable origin of our own word *ballast*.

The Saxons were good sailors and recognized an important fact—an empty ship is often less seaworthy than a loaded one. Fifteen hundred years later this fact is no less true. We still use ballast and our reasons are basically the same: 1) to increase seaworthiness and stability; 2) to equalize stresses on the hull; 3) to increase maneuverability and speed.

THE NEED FOR BALLAST

An empty tanker rides high in the water and is vulnerable to the attacks of an angry sea. Instead of slicing through the swells, the bow tends to bounce along on top of them. This action creates dangerous stresses on the ship's structure.

The ship is also less maneuverable; the propeller and rudder—only partially submerged when a tanker is "light"—lose much of their efficiency.

One obvious solution (the one tanker companies prefer) is to make sure a tanker always sails with cargo in her tanks. This not only makes her more seaworthy but more profitable too.

This arrangement is ideal but often impractical. For example, the typical VLCC can only carry cargo in one direction: from the oil fields to the refinery or receiving terminal. The long voyage outbound to the oil fields must be made with no cargo in the tanks at all.

And here is where ballast (sea water) must take the place of the missing cargo. Sea water is the logical choice because it is abundant, free, and easy to use. On older ships it is delivered into empty cargo tanks with the main cargo pumps. Special ballast lines run from the skin of the ship to the pumps. Sea valves regulate the flow of water to and from the sea.

On new ships—and some old ones—certain tanks are reserved for clean ballast only. A separate pump and pipeline are provided for ballast; the ballast system is thus kept free of oil, and only clean ballast need be pumped overboard.

PLANNING THE BALLAST LOAD

Ballasting involves more than just filling tanks with sea water; it must be carefully planned. The following factors must be considered when planning the distribution of ballast.

Stress. Generally speaking, ballast must be spread evenly through the tanks, taking care not to concentrate it in the middle or at the ends. Since more tanks are left empty when ballasting than when loading cargo, these empty tanks must be distributed carefully. Additional empty tanks increase the possibility of creating a dangerous hog or sag condition.

Stress should therefore be calculated for each ballast plan used. (Methods for checking stress are discussed in Chapter 6.)

Draft. A ballasted ship normally draws much less water than a loaded ship. The draft calculation is sometimes critical, however, as when crossing a shallow bar at low tide.

Trim. On most tankers, 4 to 10 feet of stern trim are satisfactory during a ballast passage. However, the trim must be increased during tank cleaning to improve efficiency of the stripping pumps (which are used to remove slops; see Chapter 8). At least 10 feet of trim are required for this purpose; more on large vessels.

Propeller immersion. A ship's propeller must remain submerged to operate at full efficiency. The ballast load should be planned with this fact in mind.

Weather expected on the ballast passage. Weather is a vital consideration in ballast planning. Bad weather can force a tanker to take on as much as 60 percent of her loaded deadweight in ballast; sometimes even more. In good weather this amount is naturally much less.

One of the most important things is to prevent *pounding*, which occurs when the bow crashes over oncoming swells instead of slicing through them. Enough forward draft must be maintained to keep the bow well submerged.

Tank cleaning. Whenever repairs or inspections must be made inside the tanks, they must first be cleaned and gas-freed (see Chapter 8). This operation is a routine part of the ballast passage. Tanks to be cleaned must, of course, be empty when the cleaning is performed. Ballasting should be planned with this in mind.

When more than a few tanks are to be cleaned, it is usually necessary to shift or discharge ballast from some of the ballasted tanks. This is also the case when using the load-on-top technique for ballast handling (discussed later in this chapter and in Chapter 10).

CHOOSING THE PLAN

After considering the requirements for a particular ballast load, old ballast plans should be consulted; one of these should prove adequate

Fig. 66. A 119,000-d.w.t. tanker leaves port in ballast (as viewed looking aft along the main deck). A number of tanks have already been cleaned and gas-freed (note the open ullage trunks). Also visible in this photograph: fore-and-aft walkway, cargo and steam piping on deck, automatic tapewells, fire main, steam-powered deck machinery, and tank vents. A Shell Photo.

Fig. 67. Proper ballasting of tankers increases maneuverability and speed. Kockums Automation AB.

for the present voyage. This is generally the chief mate's job, although the master may want to choose the plan himself.

Many ships keep a book of standard ballast plans which cover the whole spectrum of ballast conditions. For example, Fig. 69 illustrates a plan which might be used by a 65,000-ton tanker in moderate weather. In fair weather an arrangement such as the one shown in Fig. 70 might be used. Here, only tanks on the clean ballast system are used (forepeak, forward and after clean ballast tanks, afterpeak, three wings, five wings).

The exact figures for trim, draft, and displacement will vary each time a plan is used, depending on the amount and position of bunkers, water, and stores. Most of the time these differences are insignificant.

Fig. 68. Ballasting involves more than just filling tanks with sea water; it must be carefully planned. Chevron Shipping Company.

CLEAN BALLAST VERSUS DIRTY BALLAST

At this point we should make an important distinction between clean ballast and dirty ballast. The U.S. Coast Guard defines *clean ballast* as follows:

... ballast in a tank which, since oil was last carried in it, has been so cleaned that ballast, if discharged from a stationary vessel into clean, calm water on a clear day, would make no visible traces of oil on the water surface or adjoining shore lines or cause a sludge or emulsion to be deposited beneath the water surface or on adjoining shore lines.

S.S. SHASTA VALLEY
Ballast Plan # *3 (moderate weather)*

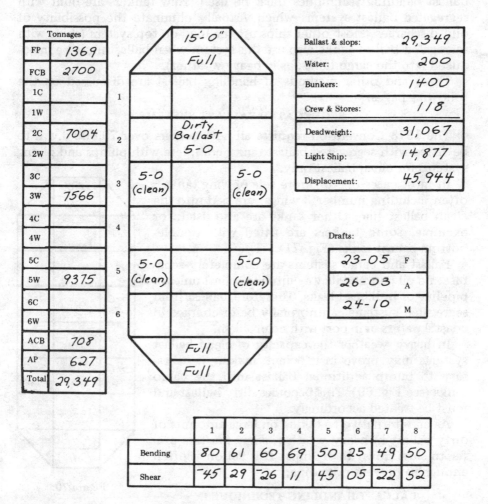

Tonnages	
FP	*1369*
FCB	*2700*
1C	
1W	
2C	*7004*
2W	
3C	
3W	*7566*
4C	
4W	
5C	
5W	*9375*
6C	
6W	
ACB	*708*
AP	*627*
Total	*29,349*

Ballast & slops:	*29,349*
Water:	*200*
Bunkers:	*1400*
Crew & Stores:	*118*
Deadweight:	*31,067*
Light Ship:	*14,877*
Displacement:	*45,944*

Drafts:

23-05	F
26-03	A
24-10	M

Tank labels in plan: 15'-0" Full; Dirty Ballast 5-0; 5-0 (clean) 5-0 (clean); 5-0 (clean) 5-0 (clean); Full; Full

	1	2	3	4	5	6	7	8
Bending	80	61	60	69	50	25	49	50
Shear	⁻45	29	⁻26	11	45	05	⁻22	52

Fig. 69. A moderate weather ballast plan for a 65,000-d.w.t. tanker.

It takes very little oil to produce a trace on the water's surface; therefore, ballast containing even a small amount of oil must not be pumped overboard in areas where this is illegal.

Laws forbid the discharge of dirty ballast within the *prohibited zones*, which normally extend 50 miles from shore (farther in some areas). Limited amounts of ballast may be discharged on the high seas beyond the prohibited zones, but this is strictly regulated too. (The amount of oil which may be discharged on the high seas is specified by the *International Convention for the Prevention of Pollution from Ships, 1973;* see Chapter 10).

In order to comply with local and international regulations, careful ballast handling techniques must be used. New tankers are built with segregated ballast systems which virtually eliminate the possibility of oily discharges. Most other ships use the load-on-top system (ships with segregated ballast tanks also use this system when ballast must be introduced into the cargo tanks, as in heavy weather).

These and other methods of handling ballast are discussed on the following pages.

SEGREGATED BALLAST SYSTEMS

The 1973 Convention requires all new tankers over 70,000 d.w.t. to be fitted with segregated ballast tanks, complete with pumps and piping systems for clean ballast only.

In most cases one or more sets of wing tanks—often including number 3 wings—are tied into the clean ballast line. Other tanks are also used; for example, some tankers are fitted with double-bottom ballast tanks (Fig. 71).

Ballast and cargo systems are completely separate: no oil can find its way into the ballast unless a pipeline or bulkhead leaks. Therefore, ballast from segregated systems can normally be discharged in coastal waters or in port with no problem.

In heavy weather the capacity of clean ballast systems may prove insufficient, making it necessary to pump additional ballast into the cargo tanks (see Fig. 69). This becomes dirty ballast and must be treated accordingly.

As an alternative to taking on large amounts of dirty ballast in heavy weather, some masters prefer to slow down their ships. This action is often enough to prevent pounding.

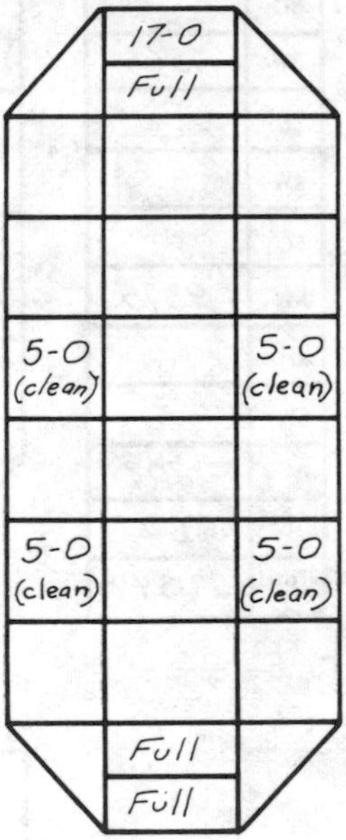

Figure 70.

BALLAST HANDLING TECHNIQUES

Many ships are either too old or too small to fall under the rule requiring separate ballast tanks. On these ships ballast must be handled with deliberate care—especially in the prohibited zones—to avoid illegal discharges of oil.

Loading dirty ballast requires all the precautions which would normally be devoted to loading cargo. A spill involving dirty ballast is no less serious than one involving cargo; in addition, risk of fire and explosion are as great, if not greater, with dirty ballast as they are with cargo.

Sea valves. Sea water is introduced into the cargo system by opening the sea valves (or *sea suctions,* as they are often called). This is a critical

Fig. 71. The *Golden Dolphin*, a 90,000-d.w.t. tanker built in 1974, is fitted with double bottom tanks for clean ballast. National Steel and Shipbuilding Company.

operation because it exposes the cargo system directly to the sea. If done incorrectly it can result in a bad spill; there is always a risk that oil will flow *out* instead of sea water flowing *in* (Fig. 72).

Normally one sea valve is located on each side of the pumproom, port and starboard. These valves sit right at the skin of the ship. When taking on ballast, only one of these valves need be opened in most cases.

Before opening the sea valve, however, it is important to check the lineup carefully. Make sure each tank valve is open in the tanks designated to receive ballast.

When ballasting through the cargo system, the main object is to prevent oil in the line from escaping as the sea valve is opened. Therefore, *always start the pump first*, before opening the sea valve. This creates a vacuum which immediately draws sea water into the line as the valve is opened. Consequently, no oil is allowed to escape.

Because sea valves are located at the bottom of the pumproom and the pump controls are often located elsewhere, a communication system must be devised between valve operator and pump operator. For example, when pumps are controlled in the engine room, a common

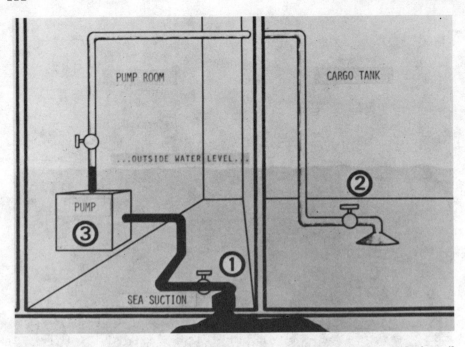

Fig. 72. When ballasting through the cargo system, there is always a risk that oil will escape through the sea suction. This can be prevented with careful ballast handling techniques. Chevron Shipping Company.

method is to pound on the pumproom bulkhead with a wrench (one knock, start number one pump; two knocks, start number two, etc.). This can be heard clearly in the engine room on the other side of the bulkhead.

Ballast is sometimes loaded by gravity without using the pumps. Tanks cannot be topped off in this manner, however, since water will stop flowing into the tanks when it reaches the level of the water surrounding the vessel. At this point the pumps must be used to take the level higher.

In any event, whether ballasting with the pumps or by gravity, the sea valve should be the last valve opened and the first valve closed.

Load-on-top (LOT). This technique was introduced on tankers in the early 1960s. It has become an almost universal practice on crude carriers and is also used on some product carriers. The following paragraphs describe how it works.

A tanker begins her ballast passage in dirty ballast. During the passage selected tanks are cleaned, then filled with sea water ballast. The bottom portion of the dirty ballast is, in the meantime, carefully pumped overboard. Providing that it has settled for a few days, this bottom water should be clean (free oil having floated to the surface). Nevertheless, it should not be discharged inside the prohibited zone, since it is bound to contain a small amount of oil.

At this point in the procedure, each dirty ballast tank contains several feet of residues; these are stripped into a single slop tank. The resultant oil-and-water mixture is allowed to settle in the slop tank for a few days, after which the clean bottom portion is pumped overboard. The remaining slops are retained and intermingled with the next cargo (which is literally "loaded on top" of the slops).

In this manner a tanker enters the prohibited zone at the end of her ballast passage with clean ballast in her tanks (except for the slops to be retained).

See Chapters 8 and 10 for a more detailed discussion of the procedures involved.

DEBALLASTING

Ballast must naturally be removed from a ship's tanks before cargo can be loaded. Clean ballast can normally be pumped overboard on the approach to the loading port or in the harbor itself, providing it produces no traces of oil on the water's surface.

Unfortunately, not all ships are able to arrive with clean ballast in their tanks. For this reason many terminals have improved their capacity to receive dirty ballast water. This has greatly simplified the task of deballasting.

Ballast is pumped ashore (into the terminal's slop line) as if it were cargo. Each tank is stripped in the usual manner by accumulating residues in a single tank. This tank is discharged last and stripped into the shore line.

Fig. 73. Birth of a VLCC: wing tank modules are positioned for final hull erection. Gigantic tanks such as these present formidable cleaning problems. The Ralph M. Parsons Company.

Chapter 8

TANK CLEANING

Early in my career as a deck officer, it was my good fortune to observe a complete tank cleaning operation on board a T2 tanker. I joined the ship in Honolulu, where she began her voyage, in ballast, to a West Coast dry dock. I took charge of the four-to-eight watch on the bridge, thus freeing the chief mate to supervise the tank cleaning. This operation was carried out round-the-clock during the nine-day passage to the shipyard.

During the previous year and a half, the ship had been in the black oil trade. Thick, waxy residues of past cargoes clung to every inner surface of her tanks.

Petroleum residues produce vapors which are both explosive and poisonous; the idea now was to clean the tanks so that upon our arrival they could be certified gas-free, "safe for men, safe for fire." This would make it possible for shipyard workers to enter and make repairs.

To me it seemed an impossible task. I watched from my vantage point on the bridge as crew members dragged hoses and portable tank cleaning machines across the foredeck. These were lowered into the tanks, tied off securely, and charged with hot sea water from the fire main. Each night I went to sleep listening to the distant echo of water cascading off bulkheads in the tanks below my room.

But washing with machines was only the first step in the process. Next began the dreaded *mucking*. I watched from the bridge as the sailors descended, one by one, into the darkness of a forward center tank. Blowers mounted in special deck openings kept a stream of fresh air flowing into the claustrophobic depths, making it possible for the men to work and breathe in safety.

One sailor remained on deck to operate a pneumatic hoist, which he positioned over the tank's ullage trunk. He sent down buckets and scoops. A short time later, he began hauling up the buckets, now full of "muck" from the tank bottom. He hauled up a lot of buckets.

After mucking, the tanks were washed again with hot, high-pressure sea water.

It all added up to a dirty, exhausting, time-consuming process—but it worked. When the ship arrived at the dry dock, a marine chemist came aboard, tested each tank, and issued the appropriate "gas-free" certificate (Fig. 75). Welders entered the tanks in short order and were soon busy making repairs.

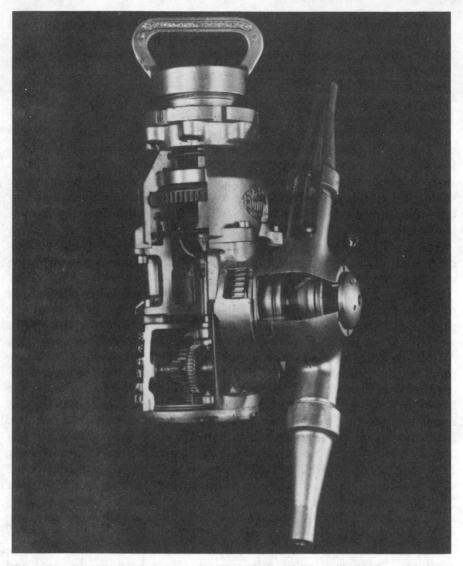

Fig. 74. *Butterworth* type "K" portable tank cleaning machine (cutaway view). Butterworth Systems, Inc.

WHY CLEAN TANKS?

Not all tank cleaning operations are as difficult as the one just described. The time and effort required, plus the method used, vary according to the previous cargo and the degree of cleanliness required. For example, it is much easier to prepare a light-oil tanker for clean ballast than a black-oil tanker for "hot" repair work inside the tanks.

The reasons for cleaning tanks include: 1) change in cargo; 2) repair work or inspection; 3) prevention of sludge accumulation; 4) preparation for clean ballast; 5) preparation for shipyard.

Like any other operation on board a tanker, the cleaning of tanks must be planned and executed carefully. An improperly cleaned tank can cause severe problems. Suppose, for example, that a consignment of stove oil is mixed with a small amount of gasoline inadvertently left in a tank. The resultant mixture could cause an explosion in somebody's home.

METHODS AND EQUIPMENT

Mechanical tank cleaning machines were first developed in the late 1920s. Prior to their introduction, and for some time afterward, tanks were cleaned by hand-hosing with salt water. Today this method is still used occasionally by ships in special trades. However, the vast majority of tank cleaning is now accomplished with machines, either fixed or portable.

Tank cleaning machines are designed to deliver sea water under high pressure in a rotating stream which arcs through every possible angle. Thus nearly all surfaces in the tank are exposed to the stream. Those not struck directly are hit by water splashing at high velocity from other parts of the tank (although it is sometimes necessary to spot clean problem areas, either by lashing a portable machine nearby or installing a special nozzle permanently in that area).

A special pump delivers sea water into the system (often employing the fire main) at pressures ranging from 100 to 190 p.s.i. Pressures are adjusted according to the type of product being cleaned from the tank. The pump is often located in the engine room; when this is the case it is necessary to call the engineers to start or stop the cleaning water or change the pressure. (On some tankers the cargo pumps can deliver into the tank cleaning system, making a special pump unnecessary.)

Sea water can either be used cold or heated to temperatures up to 190° F. (by means of a heat exchanger in the engine room). This, too, depends on the previous product and the degree of cleanliness required.

On ships carrying heavy crudes and fuel oils, for example, it is common to wash tanks at "180-180"; that is, 180 p.s.i. and 180° F. A ship carrying refined products, on the other hand, might use cold sea water at 120 p.s.i. This depends, once again, on the type of product carried and the reason for cleaning the tanks.

An increasingly popular practice is to coat the insides of cargo tanks with a special paint, thus reducing the amount of time and effort required for tank cleaning. Many tankers, especially new ones, are so fitted; this makes the job of tank cleaning much easier.

A certain amount of caution must be used when cleaning coated tanks, however. Epoxy coatings can be damaged by using excessive

(Text continues on page 122.)

MARINE CHEMIST'S CERTIFICATE

VESSEL: _____

Vessel type: _____

Tank coating mtl.: _____

Location: _____

Job for: _____

Last cargo: _____

Cert. No.: _____

Date: _____

Time: _____

Local shifting of vessel is/is not authorized.

If delay in excess of 24 hrs. before commencing work in certified spaces is authorized, circumstances shall be explained in remarks section.

COMPARTMENTS TESTED | DESIGNATIONS — QUALIFICATIONS

Fig. 75. Marine Chemist's Certificate. U.S. Coast Guard.

118

REMARKS — INSTRUCTIONS FOR MAINTAINING CONDITIONS:

In the event of any physical or atmospheric changes affecting the gas-free condition of the above spaces, or if in any doubt, immediately contact the undersigned.

CHEMIST'S ENDORSEMENT: This is to certify that I have examined all spaces in the foregoing list in accordance with the "Standard for the Control of Gas Hazards on Vessels to be Repaired," adopted by the National Fire Protection Association, and have found the condition of each to be in accordance with its assigned designation.

This certificate is based on conditions existing at the time the inspection herein set forth was completed and is issued subject to compliance with all qualifications and instructions. In the event of any steaming, cleaning, opening valves, breaking pipe lines, shifting vessel or ballast, or other activity altering conditions within the space, this certificate becomes void. Nothing in the wording of this certificate shall be interpreted as approval of hot work on the boundaries of any enclosed space not certified "safe for fire." All lines, vents, heating coils, valves and similarly enclosed appurtenances shall be considered "not safe" unless otherwise specifically designated. This certificate is not a permit.

Signed.................................

Marine Chemist   *Cert. No.*

STANDARD DESIGNATIONS

SAFE FOR MEN — SAFE FOR FIRE: Means that in the compartment or space so designated and in the adjacent compartments or spaces: (a) The gas content of the atmosphere is within a permissible concentration and that; (b) In the judgment of the Marine Chemist, the residues are not capable of producing a dangerous concentration of gases under existing atmospheric conditions in the presence of fire and while maintained as directed on the Marine Chemist's certificate. (c) If in the judgment of the Marine Chemist a test for oxygen content is necessary and made, the oxygen content of the atmosphere is at least 16.5 per cent by volume.

SAFE FOR MEN — NOT SAFE FOR FIRE: Means that in the compartment or space so designated: (a) The gas content of the atmosphere is within a permissible concentration and that; (b) In the judgment of the Marine Chemist, the residues are not capable of producing dangerous gases under existing atmospheric conditions in the presence of fire and while maintained as directed on the Marine Chemist's certificate. (c) If in the judgment of the Marine Chemist a test for oxygen content is necessary and made, the oxygen content of the atmosphere is at least 16.5 per cent by volume.

NOT SAFE FOR MEN — SAFE FOR FIRE: Means that in the judgment of the Marine Chemist, the residues in the compartment or space so designated are not combustible or flammable, but are considered hazardous to personnel. In such cases this designation shall be followed by a statement explaining the condition of this space.

NOT SAFE FOR MEN — NOT SAFE FOR FIRE: Means that in the compartment or space so designated: (a) The gas or oxygen content of the atmosphere is not within a permissible concentration, or that; (b) Dangerous gases are present or, in the judgment of the Marine Chemist, the residues are capable of producing dangerous gases under existing atmospheric conditions, or that; (c) The compartment was not tested because it contained ballast, slops, bunkers, etc. In such cases this safety designation shall be followed by a statement of the condition of the compartment which prevented it from being tested.

SAFE FOR SHIPBREAKING: Means that in the compartment or space so designated and in the adjacent compartments or spaces: (a) The gas content of the atmosphere by volume is within a permissible concentration and that; (b) In the judgment of the Marine Chemist, the residues are not capable of producing dangerous gases under existing conditions while maintained as directed on the Marine Chemist's certificate, and that; (c) If in the judgment of the Marine Chemist a test for oxygen content is necessary and made, the oxygen content of the atmosphere is at least 16.5 per cent by volume, and that; (d) Residual combustible materials within the designated compartment are not capable of producing fires beyond the extinguishing capabilities of the equipment on hand.

Fig. 75. *(cont.)*

Fig. 76. *Gunclean* fixed tank cleaning machine in action. Hudson Engineering Company.

Fig. 77. Main-deck components of the *Gunclean* 5000 R remote-controlled fixed
tank cleaning machine. Shipbuilding and Marine Engineering International.

(Continued from page 117.)
pressures or temperatures in the wash water. For example, 120 p.s.i. and 120° F. might be the maximums used on a typical ship. Generally speaking, washing times are greatly reduced when cleaning coated tanks.

Gas-freeing. Crew members must frequently enter tanks for inspection or repairs, in which case the tanks must be thoroughly ventilated after washing. Several types of portable high-capacity blowers (Fig. 79) are used; these are powered by steam, air, or water. Special openings in the main deck are fitted in various positions over each tank. When the covering plates are removed, blowers can be placed into the openings. (These openings are also used for portable tank cleaning machines.)

Newer ships are sometimes equipped with permanent fans or eductors designed to extract air through the cargo piping. Such installations normally eliminate the need for portable blowers.

Portable tank cleaning machines. Although permanently installed tank washing systems are becoming increasingly popular (they are standard equipment on VLCCs), portable machines are still used on most American ships.

Portable machines are used in conjunction with 2½″ rubber hoses, which are connected to the tank cleaning line (usually the fire main). The machines are screwed onto the hoses, then hung through tank cleaning openings in the deck. The hoses are secured in special saddles on deck or, in some cases, special hose reels are used (Fig. 80).

Although each hose supports the full weight of its machine, a separate safety line is also attached to the machine. This prevents the machine from dropping into the tank in the event of a broken or uncoupled hose and is helpful when hauling the machine out of the tank.

On smaller ships only one or two machines are operated in a tank; rarely more. The tanks are washed in a series of drops, often three, beginning near the top of the tank and working downward. The hoses are marked in 5-foot intervals to facilitate the accurate positioning of machines.

The exact height of each drop is dictated by the inner structure of the tank. On ships which have been in service for a few years, experience has

Fig. 78. *Lavomatic* fixed tank cleaning machine. Butterworth Systems, Inc.

Fig. 79. Portable high-capacity blower (shown with adapter) used for gas-freeing cargo tanks. Portable blowers are placed over tank openings on the main deck. They are normally driven by steam or compressed air. Coppus Engineering Corporation.

shown how many machines to use in a given tank, for a given length of time, to clean a given product—and at what pressure, temperature, height, and number of drops.

For example, a 16,000-ton tanker in black oil service might use two machines at 180 p.s.i. and 180° F. in the following pattern:

1st drop: 7 feet, ½ hour
2nd drop: 17 feet, ½ hour
3rd drop: 30 feet, 1 hour

By way of contrast, a 70,000-ton black-oil tanker might use four or more machines, also at 180-180, in this pattern:

1st drop: 15 feet, 1 hour
2nd drop: 30 feet, 1 hour
3rd drop: 45 feet, 2 hours

These figures are meant as examples only; they would vary considerably from ship to ship and in differing circumstances. Generally speaking, the number of minutes a machine is used at each drop depends on the amount of time required to complete one or more full cycles.

Fixed systems. In recent years the world has witnessed a magnificent increase in the size of tankers. Ships are built bigger, but with fewer tanks. This development has spurred important changes in tank cleaning methods.

Cleaning the cavernous tanks of a VLCC with portable machines would be little more effective than sending the crew inside with squirt guns. In short, a much larger machine is required, a machine too heavy

Fig. 80. Hose reel systems are sometimes used when washing with portable machines. Gamlen Chemical Company.

and awkward to drag vast distances across a VLCC's deck. The logical solution is to mount these machines permanently inside the tanks.

Such a system has numerous advantages. Machines can be put on or taken off the line simply by turning a valve; therefore, fewer men are required. This eliminates much dirty, exhausting, dangerous work—with attendant risk of dropped machines, broken feet, and bruises.

The pressure, temperature, and washing times used with fixed machines vary, just as they do with portable machines. Generally speaking, the large tanks of a VLCC take much longer to wash than those on a small product carrier. For example, a center tank might normally require eight hours.

Cleaning charts. Most tanker companies provide detailed instruction manuals and cleaning charts outlining cleaning procedures; these indicate the exact requirements when making the transition from one product to another.

As an example let's assume the last cargo carried in a tank was automobile gasoline; the new cargo, aviation gasoline. The cleaning chart would indicate that no washing is necessary between these particular products (provided that no exotic additives were used in the auto-

Fig. 81. *Gamajet II* portable tank cleaning machine. Gamlen Chemical Company.

mobile gasoline). On the other hand, the transition to a sensitive product like insulating oil might require extensive tank cleaning, hand mopping, and flushing. These procedures would be outlined on the cleaning chart.

STRIPPING AND DISPOSING OF SLOPS

Effective stripping is a vital part of tank cleaning. Wash water must be removed continuously as it enters the tanks; otherwise it quickly pools up and prevents the water stream from hitting the bottom. The bottom is the dirtiest part of a tank, with the greatest accumulation of

Fig. 82. *Gunclean* 3000/5000 W main-deck unit. Salen & Wicander AB.

sludge. It is therefore essential to keep the bottom dry, and thus exposed to the water stream, during the entire washing cycle.

One of the stripping pumps or a reciprocating main cargo pump is used for this purpose. The pump must be set at a speed equal to or slightly greater than the input of water. As a rule, this is a very slow pumping rate.

Pumps have a tendency to lose suction during tank cleaning, so it is important to watch them carefully. If water begins to pool up on the bottom of a tank, it is a fair bet the pump has lost suction. In such cases the pump must be primed from a full ballast tank or bled off as described in Chapter 5. Plenty of stern trim, at least 10 feet, is required for effective stripping.

At this point a problem arises—what to do with the slops? In the past it was common, during a ballast passage, to pump slops directly into the sea (except in prohibited areas near coastlines). This practice has ended, however. The 1973 *International Convention for the Prevention of Pollution from Ships* places strict limits on the amount of oil which may be discharged on the high seas (see Chapter 10). Slops must therefore be retained on board.

The aftermost center tank (or in some cases the aftermost pair of wing tanks) adjacent to the pumproom is most often used for this purpose. As we learned in Chapter 5, this tank is usually fitted with a special filling line from the pumproom.

As this tank fills with slops, oily residues gradually float to the surface. The water which settles at the bottom is, in most cases, clean enough to discharge overboard.

When the level of the slop tank rises above the water line, it can normally be gravitated to sea with little risk of oil going overboard (provided that adequate time has been allowed for settling). On some tankers the slop tank is opened to sea as soon as the water level rises sufficiently. The tank is then left open throughout the tank cleaning operation, thus allowing clean water to gravitate out from the bottom as dirty water is introduced. This method does not work on all ships, however, and should be used with caution.

When tank cleaning is completed, the clean bottom water from the slop tank is pumped to sea, and the dirty top portion is retained. These remaining slops can be discharged in port or mingled with the next cargo.

The latter method is used extensively on crude carriers (see Chapter 10 for further discussion of the *load-on-top* system).

Slop disposal is simpler when tanks are cleaned in port. In most cases slops can be pumped directly ashore via the terminal's slop line. The use of a slop tank on board ship is therefore unnecessary.

WATERLESS WASHING OF TANKS

An increasing number of crude carriers have adopted a tank cleaning technique which greatly reduces the amount of slop water accumulated. Tanks are washed initially with a *crude oil spray* drawn from the ship's cargo and delivered with the fixed tank cleaning machines.

This method takes advantage of the solvent properties of crude oil, which are greatly augmented by delivery in a high-pressure spray. Crude

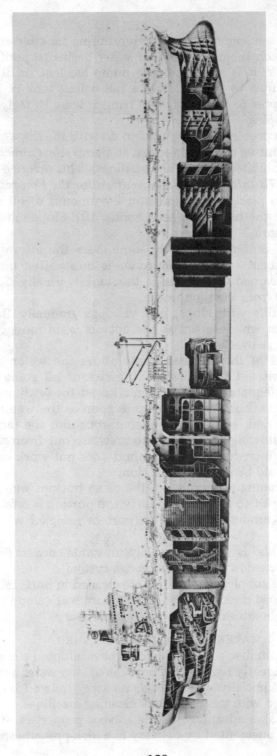

Fig. 83. Cutaway diagram of a VLCC. The immense size of cargo tanks makes washing with portable machines impractical. Instead, fixed machines much larger than portable models are installed inside the tanks. An Exxon Photo.

washing is particularly effective against built-up sludge on tank surfaces, and it significantly reduces the need for manual mucking.

Ships using this technique normally begin tank cleaning while still discharging cargo. Tanks are washed in stages. As the tank level drops, the arc of the cleaning spray is varied to "follow" the oil level downward (Fig. 84). Crude is routed from the discharge side of the cargo system into a special branch line which carries it to the tank cleaning machines. The cargo pumps supply the necessary pressure and no special pump is required.

Fig. 84. Gearbox for the *Lavomatic* fixed tank cleaning machine (installed on deck over tank). This model features a selective arc control for use with multi-stage crude washing techniques. Butterworth Systems, Inc.

The initial crude oil wash can be followed by a water rinse, if necessary. This would be done if crew members needed to enter a tank, for example. Much less water washing is required; consequently less slops are generated.

Because of the inherent risk of explosion involved with crude washing, this method can only be used by tankers fitted with inert gas systems. In addition, it is usually necessary to secure permission from port authorities before washing tanks with crude oil.

USE OF DETERGENTS AND OTHER CHEMICALS

A variety of detergents and other chemicals are available for use in tank cleaning. When added to the wash water, these substances greatly increase the speed and efficiency of the tank cleaning operation. Unfortunately, they create their own problems (which we will discuss shortly).

Detergent is commonly syphoned from drums and injected into the wash water by a portable pump. In some cases steam is injected into the tank as well. In another method solvent is mixed with the wash water, after which the slops are recirculated to the machines in a "closed" system.

Still another method employs a special nonemulsifying chemical which is sprayed full strength onto tank surfaces (Fig. 85). It is allowed to soak for several hours, after which the tank is washed with hot water in the usual manner.

Detergents and chemicals, while improving efficiency, present the following problems:

Fig. 85. A crew member sprays tank surfaces with a special chemical prior to washing with portable machines. Gamlen Chemical Company.

1. Most are poisonous and have a deadly effect on sea life. Slop water which has been treated with chemicals must therefore be retained on board, in most cases.

2. Many refineries refuse to accept slops which contain emulsifiers, detergents, and other chemicals, because of the difficulty in reprocessing such substances.

3. The addition of certain chemicals to the wash water increases the build-up of static electricity inside the tanks, especially when slops are

recirculated. As we will soon discover, static electricity can be a dangerous source of ignition in vapor-laden tanks.

LINE, PUMP, AND BOTTOM FLUSHES

When cleaning tanks it is important to remember that cargo piping is also dirty and must be flushed. This is done in a variety of ways, depending on the degree of cleanliness required.

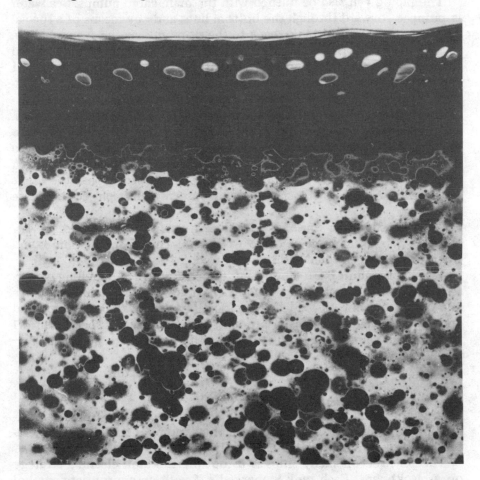

Fig. 86. Slop oil treated with a special nonemulsifying chemical quickly coalesces and floats to the surface. Gamlen Chemical Company.

Before washing tanks in preparation for clean ballast, it is essential to flush the branch lines by pumping a little water into each tank with the main cargo pumps. Otherwise the clean ballast will push the dirty contents of each branch line into the tank as it is loaded, thus contaminating the ballast. This initial flush is often performed alongside the dock before sailing on the ballast passage.

It is also wise to flush the bottom piping before pumping clean ballast overboard. Some ships are fitted with a line drop at number 1 tank for this purpose. A 2½" tank cleaning hose is hooked up to the drop, by means of a special adapter, and hot water is flushed through the system. Master valves and crossovers are arranged so that the whole lower piping system can be flushed aft into the slop tank.

The piping can also be flushed with the main cargo pumps. Sea water is pumped forward through the bottom lines and—by means of a special crossover at number 1 tank—back to the slop tank via the stripping line.

This method forms an improvised loop, with water travelling forward through the main lines and returning aft through the stripping line. It can only be used, unfortunately, on ships fitted with a forward crossover between main and stripping lines.

On light-oil ships, mainly those carrying water-sensitive cargoes, another situation sometimes arises at the loading port. Just prior to loading, the tank bottoms are occasionally flushed with the product to be loaded. An inch or two of product is loaded into each tank, then pumped ashore via the terminal's slop line. This assures that the ship's pipelines and tank bottoms are clear of water which might contaminate the cargo.

After loading has finished, the pumps can also be flushed by discharging a small amount of cargo with each. This clears the pumps and the piping between them and the manifold.

These procedures are important, especially when handling water-sensitive products. Refinery technicians take product samples before and after the ship is loaded. Specifications (such as flash point and gravity) are checked for each product. When the final "specs" fall off their initial values, the ship's officers—the chief mate in particular—usually take the blame.

Careful tank cleaning and flushing help to prevent this.

THE TANK CLEANING TEAM

It is the chief mate's job to plan the tank cleaning operation, including number and position of machines, number of drops, temperature and pressure of wash water, and flushing procedures.

The practice on many ships is to outline the tank cleaning strategy on a blackboard. Each tank is marked off with an appropriate symbol after it is washed, gas-freed, and (if necessary) mucked.

On vessels equipped with portable machines, the operation is carried out by the pumpman (who lines up the system and strips the tanks), the bos'n (who acts as foreman on deck), and two or more sailors.

In port, the mate on watch is usually in charge; at sea, the chief mate runs the show. The officers have little to do, however, if the pumpman and bos'n know their jobs and do them properly.

The procedure is different on tankers with permanent, fixed-in-place machines, in that much less physical work is required. One or two crew members can normally do the job.

DANGERS

Tank cleaning is a routine part of tanker life and there is a temptation to become complacent about it. This is a mistake; *tank cleaning is hazardous and should be regarded as such.*

Here is an example:

The crew of a tanker was cleaning tanks when one of the portable machines became fouled on an obstruction. It was necessary for a man to enter the tank and free the machine—a routine operation, no problem.

He donned a fresh air breathing apparatus and lifeline, then started down the ladder. One of his shipmates, who was tending the lifeline, leaned over the ullage trunk to check his progress. Inadvertently, the line tender allowed his cigarette lighter to slip out of his shirt pocket.

It tumbled into the tank, which—like a powder keg with no fuse—was brimming over with explosive vapors. There was a tiny spark and then, in an instant, the tank became an incinerator.

The lifeline and air hose disintegrated in the flames. The men topside could do nothing to save their shipmate. They stood by helplessly while he burned to death.

Crew members, especially officers, must never develop an easygoing attitude toward tank cleaning. It is one of the riskiest operations tankermen must perform, with the ever-present danger of: 1) explosion; 2) gassing or asphyxiation of crew members entering tanks; 3) injuries caused by falls inside tanks; 4) broken feet and toes, hot water burns, and bruises suffered by crew members while handling portable machines.

The first two dangers—explosion and gassing—are the most serious, but the others should not be ignored. I have seen enough burns, bruises, and smashed toes to attest to that. It was also my sad misfortune to be on board a tanker in dry dock when one of the yard workers fell and broke his neck inside a tank.

In short, tank cleaning is a time when all hands must remain alert and cautious.

EXPLOSION

Tankers have been prone to explosions since their development in the latter part of the 1800s. Risk of explosion is particularly great during tank cleaning.

Empty tanks—especially those in the process of being cleaned—are more often inhabited by explosive vapor mixtures than full tanks,

Fig. 87. Proof that tank cleaning is dangerous; the VLCC *Kong Haakon VII* exploded while cleaning tanks off the coast of Africa in 1969. U.S. Salvage Association.

where vapors are normally too "rich" to ignite. (See Chapter 9 for a discussion of *explosive range.*)

In general, officers and crew must strive to prevent explosive mixtures from contacting sources of ignition. This is accomplished primarily by eliminating sources of ignition (fires, sparks, burning cigarettes, static electricity) inside and in proximity to cargo tanks.

It is also possible to alter the vapor mixture inside the tanks. One method creates a "lean" atmosphere by blowing out vapors prior to and during the cleaning operation. Other ships are fitted with inert gas systems which dilute tank atmospheres with incombustible gasses from the ship's boilers.

On the following pages we will explore these explosion-prevention procedures in more detail.

STATIC ELECTRICITY

During an 18-day period in December of 1969, a chain of three supertanker explosions shocked the shipping world. One ship, the 206,000-ton *Marpessa*, sank as a result of the damage to her hull. At the time, she was the largest ship ever lost through sinking. The other two ships, the *Mactra* and the *Kong Haakon VII*, were salvaged and repaired at tremendous expense.

All three ships were new at the time of the explosions. In addition, all three were about the same size, all were steaming through the tropics in a ballasted condition, and *all were cleaning tanks at the time of the explosions.*

A few months after these explosions occurred, I was in San Francisco at a company meeting for ship's officers. An executive showed our group an aerial photograph taken after the explosion on board the *Mactra.* The steel deck had peeled back, like a giant sardine can, through half the length of the ship.

"This," he said, pointing at a small outline superimposed on the photograph, "indicates the approximate size of a T2 tanker. Most of you gentlemen have sailed on a T2 so you are familiar with the size. As you can see, a T2 would fit inside the hole in the *Mactra's* deck."

What had caused these disasters?

Shipowners, with millions of dollars and the lives of their crews at stake, launched an extensive investigation. Although the exact cause of the explosions will, in all likelihood, never be known, the investigation revealed evidence pointing to *static electricity* as a probable cause of ignition.

The effects of static electricity are familiar to virtually everyone. Try shuffling across a carpet and touching somebody with your fingertip. More often than not, you will each receive a tiny shock.

This is static electricity. It is caused by the tendency of electrons to transfer between molecules of unlike charge. The molecules on the soles of your shoes pick up extra electrons as you shuffle across the carpet, giving your body a negative charge. These electrons immediately want to flow toward a neutral or positively charged object, such as your unsuspecting friend across the room.

The same process takes place in the molecules of tank wash water. The water rushes through an intricate system of pipes, ejects from a whirling nozzle, and collides at tremendous velocity with the bulkheads and decks of the tank. In the process it picks up an electrical charge and leaves an opposite charge on surfaces it has contacted, such as tank cleaning machines. This action is greatly exaggerated in large tanks with huge, permanently-installed machines.

When electrons jump from one object to another, they create a *spark*. This generates heat—enough heat to ignite a flammable mixture. However, *two* things are required before a tank explosion can occur: 1) a flammable mixture of vapor and oxygen; 2) a source of ignition.

Since the *Marpessa-Mactra-Kong Haakon* explosions, many ship-owners have decided the first condition is easier to control. As a result nearly all new supertankers are being built with inert gas systems. In addition, some older ships are being converted.

Nevertheless, it is important to control the second condition—sources of ignition—whether a ship is fitted with inert gas or not. As a result of the shipowners' investigation, certain precautions have been recommended for eliminating static electricity as a source of ignition while tank cleaning.

Keep machines grounded. A clear electrical pathway must be maintained between portable machines and ground, in order to neutralize any charges which might accumulate.

Tank cleaning hoses contain one or more internal bonding wires for this purpose. As long as these wires remain intact and the hose remains securely coupled to the hydrant, electrical charges will flow freely to ground.

If, on the other hand, the electrical continuity is interrupted (as by a defective bonding wire or uncoupled hose) the electrical charge may flow the other way by *sparking into the tank*.

Crew members must not be allowed to uncouple hoses while machines are still inside the tanks. Unfortunately, some sailors are in the habit of uncoupling hoses as an easy way of draining them. *This is extremely dangerous—don't allow it.* Instead, have crew members loosen the hose coupling just enough to break the vacuum, then re-tighten after the hose has drained.

Charged steam and mist. Steam which has been injected into a tank is likely to contain a strong electrostatic charge. No objects, grounded or otherwise, should be lowered into a tank containing steam.

The same precautions should be observed immediately after cleaning a tank with water, when the charged mist suspended inside could easily spark to a foreign object. Ventilate the tank thoroughly before lowering sounding rods or other objects.

INERT GAS SYSTEMS

Until comparatively recent times, tankermen had little or no control over the atmosphere within cargo tanks. This is one of the reasons why tankers have been vulnerable to explosions since their early history, at the rate of about a dozen explosions per year.

Tanker owners have sought to remedy this situation through the use of tank inerting systems which pipe the ship's flue gasses to the cargo tanks (Fig. 88). These systems are expensive, but they work. Not a single inerted ship has suffered a cargo tank explosion, and inert gas systems are rapidly becoming standard equipment on new VLCCs.

In a ship's boiler, air (approximately 79 percent nitrogen, 21 percent oxygen) mixes rapidly with fuel oil to produce heat and the following residual gasses:

oxygen	3-4%
carbon dioxide	13%
sulphur oxides	0.3%
water vapor	5%
nitrogen	77%
other gasses	1-2%

This residual mixture is, for all practical purposes, inert and will not promote combustion. On ships fitted with inert gas systems, these gasses are drawn off, filtered of impurities, and cooled (Fig. 89). The result is a mixture of nitrogen, carbon dioxide, and about 3 percent oxygen (well below the 9 percent which is considered safe).

Fans blow this gas into the tanks by means of the regular vent system. Entering gas dilutes and displaces flammable mixtures which might be present. Thereafter, most systems automatically maintain a slight, constant pressure of gas. In this way a consistently fireproof atmosphere is sustained. Little or no air can leak in, and chances of explosion are almost nil.

ENTERING THE TANKS

I vividly remember the first time I went inside a ship's tank. I was a brand new third mate at the time.

The tank had just been washed and ventilated, tested for gas, and pronounced safe. The chief mate had climbed over the edge of the ullage trunk and was starting down the ladder when he paused and signalled me to follow.

"Come on down; you might as well get used to it."

I followed him down the ladder. It was the center tank of a T2, tiny by modern standards but still impressive. My feeling was one of entering a vast dungeon, dark, forbidding, mysterious. As we reached the bottom, I suppressed a claustrophobic urge to flee back to the sunlight which filtered dimly through the tank openings far above.

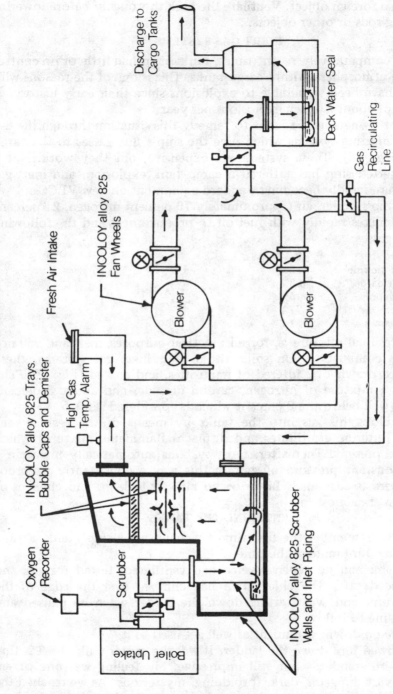

INERT GAS SYSTEM

Oxygen Recorder

Scrubber

INCOLOY alloy 825 Trays.
Bubble Caps and Demister

Fresh Air Intake

High Gas Temp. Alarm

INCOLOY alloy 825
Fan Wheels

Blower

Blower

Boiler Uptake

INCOLOY alloy 825 Scrubber
Walls and Inlet Piping

Discharge to Cargo Tanks

Deck Water Seal

Gas Recirculating Line

Fig. 88. Schematic diagram of a typical inert gas system. Huntington Alloys, Inc.

138

But my feeling of discomfort gradually disappeared as I followed the mate through the tank. It was very dark; without our flashlights we would have been lost. We inched along a precariously narrow frame, climbed over a large I-beam (the keel), and lowered ourselves onto the main cargo piping on the bottom.

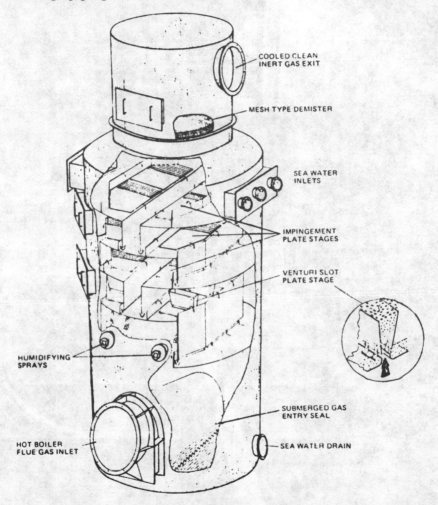

Fig. 89. Inert gas *scrubber*, used to cool the gas and remove impurities. Sun Shipbuilding and Dry Dock Company.

I was amazed at how clean everything was—rusty, but clean. The tank cleaning machines had done a thorough job.

We followed the main piping aft to a bulkhead, where a shorter section of pipe branched off to the side. At the end of this branch line sat a large gate valve from which the piping spread over the bottom in a

Fig. 90. Both man and machine are dwarfed by the dimensions of a modern cargo tank. Salen & Wicander AB.

bellmouth. I spotted a separate, smaller pipeline and valve nearby: this was the stripping line.

The mate checked everything with his flashlight—valves, piping, reach rods—and jotted a few things in his notebook.

"You know," he said, looking up from his notes, "I almost died in one of these tanks. It was about a year ago. I started feeling a little dizzy, didn't think much of it, and kept on working. Next thing I knew, I was up on deck vomiting."

"What happened?" I asked.

"There was gas in the tank—I passed out."

"Gas?"

"Petroleum vapors, very poisonous. The worst thing is you don't even know it's happening—no smell, nothing. You just pass out. A few minutes later you're dead."

"But they pulled you out in time."

"I was lucky. The second mate knew how to use the breathing apparatus and he got down there right away. Otherwise I wouldn't be here."

TWO BASIC DANGERS

This was no idle warning.

Every time a tankerman descends into a tank, there is a chance he won't come out alive. The ill-informed and the foolhardy are the most likely to perish. It is therefore essential to understand both the risks and precautions involved.

Besides the risk of fire and explosion which we have already discussed, two basic dangers lurk inside empty cargo tanks: 1) *gassing*—caused by breathing poisonous hydrocarbon vapors; 2) *asphyxiation*—caused by lack of oxygen.

Gassing. Petroleum vapors are poisonous. Even low concentrations can kill a human being in minutes. The gassing victim first feels a slight dizziness, followed by a mild elation. He quickly loses his sense of smell, begins to feel drunk, slurs his speech, staggers, becomes increasingly confused, loses consciousness, and—unless removed to fresh air in short order—dies.

This all happens very quickly. Some gasses, such as hydrogen sulfide, can render a man unconscious after two or three inhalations. Hydrogen sulfide, which is found in Arabian crude and other so-called "sour" crudes, is characterized by a "rotten egg" odor in small concentrations. However, in higher concentrations it has virtually no odor, because *hydrogen sulfide like all hydrocarbon vapors quickly deadens the sense of smell.*

Before entering a tank, always check the vapor content with a combustible gas indicator (Fig. 91). The indicator draws a sample of the tank atmosphere by means of a "sniffer" attached to a long tube.

This sample should be taken close to the bottom of the tank, where petroleum vapors (which are heavier than air) are most likely to accumulate. Concentrations of vapor should also be suspected near bell-mouths, corners, beam faces, and puddles of oil or sludge.

Combustible gas indicators are designed to detect explosive concentrations of vapor. However, petroleum vapors are poisonous in concentrations well below the lower explosive limit (the L.E.L., about 1-2 percent for most products).

Therefore, the slightest movement of the needle indicates an unsafe condition.

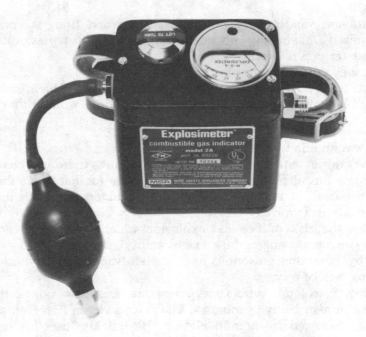

Fig. 91. Combustible gas indicator *(Explosimeter)*. Mine Safety Appliances Company.

Important notes on combustible gas indicators follow.

1. They detect vapor at the point of the sample only. Pockets of vapor may be present in other parts of the tank.

2. They do not work properly in oxygen-deficient atmospheres. They may indicate a safe condition when, in fact, a high concentration of vapor is present along with a deficiency of oxygen. When in doubt, use an oxygen indicator.

Tanks should be retested at frequent intervals, hourly if necessary, while crew members are working inside. In addition, *tanks must be ventilated continuously while crew members are below.*

Muck, sludge, and scale give off vapors which can quickly gas up a tank. Crew members walking through puddles of oil or sludge may accelerate this process. Leaky fittings such as pipelines, valves, and heating coils can also introduce vapors.

If you suspect a tank is gassing up, get out immediately. But remember—don't rely on your nose for warning.

Asphyxiation. Human beings quickly perish without oxygen. A compartment containing less than 18 percent oxygen by volume is unsafe.

Permanent ballast tanks, cofferdams, chain lockers, peak tanks, and other sealed spaces may become deficient in oxygen as a result of the

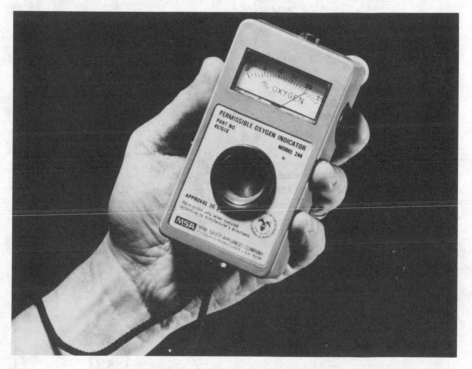

Fig. 92. Oxygen indicator. Mine Safety Appliances Company.

rusting process, which consumes oxygen. Tanks which have been inerted may be equally hazardous. Such spaces should be thoroughly ventilated before crew members are allowed to enter.

It is always a good idea to check the air inside with an oxygen indicator (Fig. 92). A reading under 18 percent indicates insufficient oxygen, and you must ventilate the compartment until a safe reading is achieved.

Precautions. The following precautions should be observed when entering tanks:

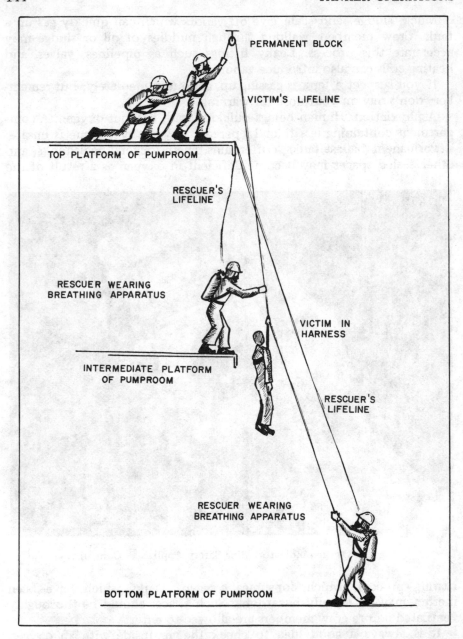

Fig. 93. Proper method of making a pumproom rescue. Speed is essential in both pumproom and tank rescues: the victim must be removed to fresh air within 4 to 6 minutes to prevent permanent brain damage or death. U.S. Coast Guard.

Fig. 94. The compressed air type of breathing apparatus has become
increasingly popular on tankers; it is fast and simple to use. Mine Safety
Applicances Company.

1. Check for petroleum vapors before entering. Don't rely on smell;
use an *Explosimeter* or similar device. The slightest movement of the
needle denotes an unsafe atmosphere.

2. Make sure oxygen content is adequate (at least 18 percent).

3. Operate blowers continuously while crew members are below.

4. Have rescue equipment close by the tank entrance and ready for
immediate use.

5. Assign somebody to remain topside and keep an eye on workers
below. Should trouble develop in the tank (men begin to pass out, for
example), his job is to *sound the alarm first,* before attempting a rescue.

GASOLINE, MOTOR

Synonyms Unavailable

Formula C_5H_{12} to C_9H_{20}

Appearance-Odor Colorless to
straw-white liquid; sweet,
pleasant odor
Specific Gravity 0.72 - 0.76
Chemical Family Hydrocarbons

Boiling Point (°F)........... 100-400
Vapor Pressure 20°C (mmHg)... 190
Reid Vapor Pressure (psia)... 7.4
Vapor Density (Air = 1)...... 3-4
Freezing Point (°F).......... Unavailable
Solubility in Water.......... Negligible

FIRE & EXPLOSION HAZARD DATA

Grade
General All petroleum hydrocarbons burn when heated above their fire point.
Dangerous fire and explosion hazard in presence of heat or flame.

Flash Point (°F) .... -40
Flammable Limits....... 1.4 - 7.6%
Autoignition Temp. (°F).. 495
Extinguishing Media ..... CO_2, dry chemical, foam, water fog
Special Fire Procedures... Tanks exposed to fire should be kept cool with a
water spray.

HEALTH HAZARD DATA

Health Hazard Ratings	Odor Threshold (ppm)	TLV (ppm)
1,1,2	Unavailable	500-1000

General Liquid irritating to skin and eyes on contact. Vapor inhalation leads
to intoxication.

Symptoms Inhalation: marked vertigo, inability to walk a straight line,
hilarity, incoordination intense burning in throat and lungs, possibly
bronchopneumonia, nausea, vomiting.
Short Exposure Tolerance 0.5 to 1.6% vapor concentration was fatal to a man after
5 minutes exposure; 500 to 30,000 ppm was fatal to a youth.

Exposure Procedures Inhalation: immediately remove victim from contaminated
atmosphere. If breathing is interrupted, artificial respiration should be
applied immediately. A physician should be called.

REACTIVITY DATA

Stability Chemically stable

Compatibility
  Material: Almost any usual material of construction is suitable. Natural
            rubber is softened and will deteriorate rapidly.
  Cargo: Group 12 of Compatibility chart.

SPILL OR LEAK PROCEDURE

Wear rubber gloves, face shield, protective clothing. Have all-purpose
canister mask available. Secure ignition sources. Small spills may be
flushed away with water. Call fire department and the nearest Captain of
the Port, U.S. Coast Guard. For a major spill, also notify State water
pollution or public health agency.

Remarks:
CG-388/1-8-73

119

Fig. 95. Sample page from *CG-388, Chemical Data Guide for Bulk
Shipment by Water.* U.S. Coast Guard.

6. If at any time while working in a tank you begin to feel dizzy or giddy, leave the space immediately. Have other crew members do the same.

RESCUE

The following equipment should be available for tank and pump-room rescues: 1) lifeline; 2) harness; 3) self-contained breathing apparatus.

The pumproom is the most frequent source of gassing accidents. One set of equipment should therefore be kept at the top of the pumproom at all times. Another set should be available for tank rescues.

Practice using the rescue equipment before you run into an emergency. When one of your shipmates passes out in a tank or pumproom, seconds count. Don't waste them reading instructions on the breathing apparatus or trying to figure out how to rig the lifeline. Learn these things beforehand.

Speed is essential. If the victim remains below longer than 4 to 6 minutes, he will suffer brain damage and, in all probability, death. Four minutes is not much time. Even a well trained rescue team working with good equipment laid out ahead of time (not always the practice, unfortunately) may have only a poor chance of success.

The situation is particularly bleak on VLCCs. A man climbing around in a VLCC center tank is little more conspicuous than a flea and, if unconscious, just as hard to find.

Noel Mostert paints an apt picture in his book, *Supership:*

... to reach someone lying in the remoter regions of the tank, lost from sight and with only a rough idea where he might be, was tantamount, surely, to being told atop the dome of a darkened Gothic cathedral to descend an eighteen-inch-wide stairway pinned to its walls and buttresses and to find somewhere at the bottom among the naves, bays, chapels, colonnades, and apses a senseless form that had to be brought aloft, all within four minutes.

The breathing apparatus is an essential part of any rescue; don't go down without one. To illustrate: try climbing out of a tank sometime while holding your breath; then imagine what it would be like with a 200-pound man on your back. It would be virtually impossible. You would have to breathe and, in all likelihood, would also succumb to the vapors.

Don't try to be a hero. Too many tankermen have died that way.

Along the same line, don't remove your air mask to give air to the victim unless an unavoidable delay makes it necessary. The important thing is to get him out quickly. Don't take time to be gentle, even if he has broken bones.

Check the victim's pulse and breathing as soon as you have him out of the tank. If his heart has stopped, pound sharply on his chest once or twice. Administer cardiopulmonary resuscitation if you know how.

If the victim has stopped breathing, apply artificial respiration. When he begins breathing on his own, have him lie face downward, with his head slightly downhill. This position will prevent him from gagging if he vomits. It will also keep his lungs clear and minimize the chance of pneumonia.

PETROCHEMICALS AND OTHER HAZARDOUS PRODUCTS

Some petroleum products are relatively harmless. Others—deadly poisons—manifest truly frightening qualities. As a final note on tank cleaning, I would like to tell a little story which should serve as a warning to new tankermen.

I was second mate of a coastwise "drug store" tanker which carried a wide variety of refined products. We had discharged a load of petrochemicals, mainly benzene, at a port near San Francisco, and were preparing to clean tanks for the back-load.

The chief mate had warned me not to breathe the cargo vapors and to keep the ullage plugs down whenever possible. Other than that, nobody seemed worried. I didn't see any reason to worry either.

I finished my watch at four in the morning and went to bed. My room was in the midship house, and since it was a hot night, I had left my porthole open. As I lay in bed, I could hear the sailors working on the foredeck. They had finished washing number 4 center and were rigging blowers to gas-free the tank. They were making a lot of noise, but it didn't bother me. Within five minutes I was asleep.

About an hour later I woke up feeling dizzy. My head throbbed. A funny, sweet smell filled the room. *What was going on?*

I staggered to my porthole and surveyed the foredeck. The gang was still gas-freeing number 4 center. A cloud of vapor, spewing from the blowers on deck, had completely enveloped the midship house—and my room.

This was common while gas-freeing number 4, but I had never before been stupid enough to leave my porthole open (portholes should always be kept closed in port). And what a time to make the mistake—benzene!

I remembered the chief mate's warning: The vapors from benzene were poisonous. In what way, I didn't know. I decided to look it up. I found a reference manual and read the following:

Benzene: Severe cumulative action when inhaled. Causes irreparable damage to blood-forming organs of the body. Dangerous in amounts over 25 parts per million.

I had been breathing a deadly poison!

By all means, you should avoid making a similar mistake. Familiarize yourself with the products you are handling. An excellent reference book is *CG-388, Chemical Data Guide for Bulk Shipment by Water*, published by the U.S. Coast Guard (Fig. 95).

Chapter 9

FIRE FIGHTING AND FIRE PREVENTION

Fire!

The word strikes fear in the hearts of tankermen, especially those who have seen a tanker burn. These men have felt the panic and desperation that only a fire at sea can cause.

But a shipboard fire need not end in tragedy. Calm, resolute, and intelligent action can defeat the most terrible conflagrations. An amazing example of this was provided by the crew of the 8,000-ton British tanker *San Demetrio* during World War II. While steaming in an Atlantic convoy, the *San Demetrio* was shelled and badly damaged by the German pocket battleship *Admiral Scheer*. Fire engulfed the tanker, which was carrying a full cargo of gasoline. It is not surprising that the crew quickly decided to abandon ship.

They drifted in the Atlantic for 20 hours. No help arrived; they had been given up for lost. Then the badly scarred hull of the *San Demetrio*, still ablaze, drifted back into view. Faced with a lack of other alternatives, the crew decided to reboard the burning vessel in the hope of saving her.

They climbed aboard with tremendous difficulty and, after two frightening days, succeeded in extinguishing the fire. Eventually the *San Demetrio* limped into port and delivered most of her valuable cargo to the Allied war effort.

More than one tanker crew has chosen to abandon ship before making a serious attempt to fight a fire. Abandoning ship is a perilous undertaking in itself, especially in rough weather. The safer alternative is often to stand fast and fight the fire. As the crew of the *San Demetrio* demonstrated, even a serious fire can, with calmness and courage, be fought successfully.

Modern tankers are supplied with fire-fighting equipment which is at once sophisticated and reliable. But even the most expensive equipment is useless if crew members are ignorant of its use.

A tanker can, at any moment, turn into a floating incinerator and, worse, a coffin for you and your shipmates. A small spark, a mislaid cigarette—it doesn't take much. You must be ready to act decisively if the unthinkable should happen.

Learn the location and function of every piece of fire-fighting equipment. This knowledge is crucial on any ship, and especially so on a tanker.

Fig. 96. Crew members practice with portable foam equipment during fire drill.
Photo by The British Petroleum Co. Ltd.

Fig. 97. This tanker, the *Salem Maritime*, was gutted by fire in 1956. U.S. Salvage
Association.

WHAT IS FIRE?

Fire. Centuries ago, human beings first learned to harness its magic power. It cooks our food, warms our homes, and powers our machines. Without it, civilization could not exist as we know it.

But fire can be a danger as well as an asset, as the caveman who discovered it undoubtedly learned. Fire burns people, too. It burns their homes, their farms, their cities. It is dangerous in other ways as well. It uses oxygen and causes asphyxiation; creates carbon monoxide, thick smoke, and toxic gasses, all of which can quickly kill.

In short, fire has been a boon to mankind but also a source of immeasurable suffering.

Fire, a chemical reaction. When vapors given off by a flammable substance combine rapidly with oxygen, we witness the phenomenon we call "fire." For example, the wax in a candle—the fuel—must first melt and then vaporize before it can be drawn into the flame and burned.

Fire is, in effect, a chemical reaction. Molecules of hydrocarbon gas join violently with molecules of oxygen to form carbon dioxide, water vapor, and most importantly, heat.

THE ELEMENTS OF FIRE

Every fire owes its existence to four indispensable elements:

1. **Fuel.** This is the vapor from petroleum or other combustibles which combines with oxygen to produce fire.

2. **Heat.** Hydrocarbon molecules must be heated substantially before they will combine with oxygen. For example, a piece of wood left lying in a cold fireplace will not ignite, but apply a sufficient amount of heat (as with burning newspapers) and it bursts into flame.

Heat need not be applied with an open flame, however. Heat can transfer through a steel bulkhead and ignite a tank of fuel oil without the aid of an open flame. This process is known as *conduction*. Heat also spreads by *convection*—the tendency of hot air to expand and move from one location to another—and by direct *radiation* (much as the sun heats a sandy beach on a summer day).

Once ignited, a fire produces its own heat and continues getting hotter, often reaching temperatures above 2,000° F. (1,100° C.).

3. **Oxygen.** People and fires both need oxygen to survive. The earth's atmosphere contains approximately 21 percent oxygen by volume. Lower this figure far enough (to 10-15 percent) and you literally "suffocate" the most tenacious fire.

4. **Chain reaction.** Molecules must pass through several steps in the oxidation process, one after another, in a regular progression. This is a little like building a tower out of toy blocks. Remove one of the blocks, and the whole structure collapses.

Fig. 98. Kings Point midshipmen attack a blaze at fire-fighting school. National
Maritime Union of America.

Similarly, remove one step from the molecular chain reaction, and a fire ceases to burn.

To extinguish a fire, therefore, at least one of four elements—fuel, heat, oxygen, chain reaction—must be removed. Modern fire-fighting equipment and methods have been developed with this fact in mind.

IMPORTANT TERMS

To aid in preventing fires and, when necessary, in extinguishing them, tankermen should understand the following terms:

Flash point is the temperature at which petroleum vapors form a flammable mixture with air. For many petroleum products (such as gasoline), the flash point is below the average temperature found in cargo tanks. In other words, you can assume explosive vapors are present when such products are carried.

Explosive range, or flammable limits. Hydrocarbon vapors will not burn in an atmosphere containing less than 10 percent oxygen. In addition, the vapors must fall within a given volumetric percentage or no reaction can take place. A mixture containing too much or too little vapor will not burn (see Table 9).

Table 9

FLAMMABLE LIMITS

(percent by volume in air)

Product	Lower Limit	Upper Limit
Crude Oils (average)	1.0	10.0
Gasoline	1.3	7.6
Kerosene	0.7	6.0
Propane	2.1	9.5
Methane	5.0	15.0
Benzene	1.4	8.0
JP4 (military jet fuel)	1.4	7.6
Ethylene Oxide	2.0	100.0

When vapors are present in amounts above the upper flammable limit, the mixture is said to be too *rich* to burn. If below the lower limit, it is too *lean*. Oddly enough, an empty tanker is more likely to fall within these dangerous limits than a full one. In fact, most tank explosions occur in empty or ballasted vessels. On vessels with full tanks, the mixture is generally well above the upper flammable limit: too rich to ignite.

This was apparently the case when, in October of 1970, the *Pacific Glory* collided with the *Allegro* off the Isle of Wight. The *Pacific Glory*, a 77,000-ton tanker fully laden with Nigerian crude, suffered severe

Fig. 99. Applying dry chemical to a *Class B* fire. Seafarers International Union.

Fig. 100. Spraying foam on an oil fire. Seafarers International Union.

engine room explosions. Fire engulfed and destroyed her superstructure and spread to the surrounding water. Nevertheless, her cargo remained untouched; it was eventually delivered to its destination in Europe.

Ignition temperature. Any flammable substance will ignite when heated sufficiently. The point at which this happens is called the ignition temperature. For petroleum products this is anywhere from 490° to 765° F. (255°-405° C.).

When heated to its ignition temperature, a product will ignite without the aid of a spark or other external source of ignition. Once ignited, a fire produces its own heat and continues to get hotter, reaching temperatures hundreds of degrees above the ignition temperature.

This fact underlines the paramount importance of *speed* in fighting fires. An incipient, relatively cool fire is much easier to extinguish than a white-hot blaze several hours in the making.

THEORY OF FIRE FIGHTING

Every fire must be attacked by removing one of the four elements previously described: fuel, heat, oxygen, or chain reaction. The extinguishing method chosen depends on the size and location of the fire, and the combustible material involved.

Table 10 lists the various classes of fire and the preferred extinguishing methods for each.

Table 10

CLASSES OF FIRE

Class	Material	Extinguishing Method/Agent
A	Ordinary combustibles such as wood, paper, and canvas.	Cooling with water or water fog. Foam, CO_2, halons, and all-purpose dry chemical are less effective but can be used.
B	Flammable liquids such as fuel oil, kerosene, and gasoline.	Smothering with foam, CO_2, inert gas, or steam. Dry chemical and halons are also effective.
C	Live electrical equipment.	Extinguishing agent must be nonconducting: CO_2, halons, dry chemical. *Water and foam must not be used.*

Removing fuel. In theory, removal of fuel is an excellent method of fighting fires, but on tankers carrying thousands of tons of petroleum it is usually impractical. Nevertheless, certain situations demand that this method be used.

For example, a fire on deck is being fed by an overflowing tank. This situation obviously calls for an immediate cessation of loading. Other, less obvious circumstances sometimes arise when the removal of fuel is indicated, so never dismiss this method as a possible means of fighting a fire.

Fig. 101. The CO_2 room. The gas is released by remote control, then carried by pipes to the protected areas. The device in the upper right-hand corner is a time release mechanism, which gives crew members time to evacuate spaces before they are flooded with CO_2. The Ansul Company.

Removing heat. Water is one of the most effective cooling agents known to man. When sprayed on a fire, it quickly turns to steam, thereby absorbing and carrying away heat.

Water is most useful on *Class A* fires since it can penetrate to the hot core of burning material. Certain other extinguishing agents—foam and steam, for example—have cooling properties, but their effect is minimal when compared to that of water.

Removing oxygen. Fires, like people, perish without oxygen. It follows that a fire can be extinguished by: 1) diluting the oxygen content until it falls below the amount necessary for combustion (10-15 percent); 2) smothering the surface of the flame so oxygen cannot enter.

Generally speaking, the first method employs carbon dioxide, steam, or inert gas; the second, mechanical foam.

Interrupting the chain reaction. Fire remains something of a mystery to scientists. They have theorized that combustion involves a rapid chain of chemical reactions without which no fire could burn. This theory seems to explain the success of dry chemical and halogenated extinguishing agents in fighting fires. These agents somehow interrupt the vital chain reaction in a fire, thus bringing on its quick demise. Research continues in this field and fire-fighting agents of this type may assume a major role in the future.

FIRE PREVENTION

The best fire is one that never happens. Such a fire can destroy no cargo or equipment, can burn no crew members, can in fact do no damage at all.

Fires are easy to start but extremely difficult to extinguish; therefore the obvious solution is to prevent them from starting. The first step in fire prevention is to *remain fire conscious at all times while on board a tanker.*

Smoking is the number-one cause of fires at sea. Many of these fires occur in the living spaces where they are extinguished before much damage is done. Some are serious, however, and one example is a tanker's captain who went to bed one night with a bottle of whisky and a lighted cigarette—a bad combination. Some time later, crew members noted a large quantity of smoke billowing out of the bridge voice tube leading to the master's cabin. They rushed below, but were too late. The "old man" was dead from asphyxiation and smoke inhalation.

Never allow yourself or the men under you to become lax about smoking rules. Encourage crew members to leave their cigarettes in their rooms or other safe areas. This precaution prevents an individual from lighting up a cigarette in an unsafe area. Only safety matches should be used; cigarette lighters should not be allowed on board.

Areas considered safe for smoking while at sea may be extremely hazardous in port. An example is the fantail. Vapors from the dock make smoking in such places a definite hazard—something crew members may not realize. The risk is particularly great after a long voyage during which the crew has become accustomed to smoking in these areas. Be alert for crew members who may "light up" without thinking.

The pumproom. If a single place on tankers can be labelled the most dangerous, it is the pumproom. Pumprooms are frequent sources of fire and explosion. In addition, many tankermen have died after being overcome by toxic pumproom vapors. Therefore, never allow yourself to become complacent about entering or working in the pumproom.

Fig. 102. Main-deck fire station. Chevron Shipping Company.

Here is an example of a man who could have used this advice:

A new pumpman was packing a leaky valve in a tanker's pumproom. At the time, the ship was carrying a full cargo of casinghead gasoline, one of the most volatile products carried on tankers. The pumpman decided to take a break and moved to a corner well away from the leaky valve. He sniffed the air, detected no gassy smell, and lit a cigarette.

A moment later he was engulfed in flames as the pumproom exploded. He was lucky, however; although badly burned, he lived to tell the tale.

There are two lessons to be learned from this episode:

1. Never trust your nose to detect petroleum vapors.

2. Always assume an explosive atmosphere exists in the pumproom.

Pumproom bilges are rarely dry, especially on older ships. It is a common practice to drain pumps and lines into the bilges; leaky fittings contribute their share as well. On very old ships the pumproom can become like a tropical rain forest of dripping oil and leaky steam lines.

Gasoline and other volatile products evaporate quickly, especially when spread across the pumproom bilge plating. The resultant vapor is both toxic and explosive. It is therefore imperative to use great care when descending into the pumproom, and to make sure the ventilation system is operating while crew members are below.

Cleaning with gasoline. Never use gasoline as a cleaning solvent. The temptation is sometimes great, particularly with thousands of gallons readily available.

On one tanker, a crew member succumbed to this temptation and caused a catastrophe. He poured a bucket of gasoline into a washing machine (which was located inside the after house) and proceeded to do his laundry. Several men were smoking nearby. Soon the machine's turbulent action generated a large amount of vapor, which spread through the accommodation area.

The subsequent explosion and fire killed four men, injured six. One of these men, his clothes ablaze, ran screaming onto the main deck. Like a human torch, he ignited four cargo tanks, one at a time, as he ran past.

Needless to say, gasoline should not be used for cleaning.

Vapor accumulations on deck. When loading in calm weather, petroleum vapor leaving the vent lines may settle around the main deck. Being heavier than air, it tends to lie close to the deck in a stagnant, invisible pool until dissipated by the wind.

This vapor may eventually find its way into living spaces, contact a source of ignition, and flash back to the tanks. The result would be explosion, fire, or both.

The hazard is greatest when handling gassy products. One ship, for example, was loading butane blend when she suffered a massive explosion. Vapor had drifted into the crew quarters, contacted a burning cigarette, and flashed back through an open ullage plug to one of the tanks. The explosion and fire which followed killed 13 men and completely destroyed the ship.

Several precautions help to avert this kind of tragedy:

1. Keep ullage plugs closed whenever possible.

2. When ullage plugs must be left open for any length of time, use a *flame screen*. This is a piece of fine wire gauze which fits over the ullage hole. A flame screen permits the passage of vapor, but not of flame.

3. Keep all doors, portholes, and other accommodation area openings fronting the cargo deck closed during cargo or ballasting operations.

4. Stop loading operations whenever heavy concentrations of vapor accumulate in the cargo handling area. This is most likely to happen on hot, humid days with no wind.

Sources of ignition. Watch for situations which could bring a spark or open flame in contact with flammable vapors. Keep a careful eye on visitors: people unfamiliar with tankers are liable to "light up" in prohibited smoking areas.

Make sure no unauthorized electrical equipment or other spark producing devices are used around cargo tanks, in the pumproom, or in other gassy areas. Carefully watch all activities on the dock. An automobile or burning cigarette on the dock could ignite low-lying vapors. In turn, these could flash back to the ship's tanks and cause an explosion.

The close approach of a tug or other vessel during cargo operations is equally hazardous. Hot, smoldering soot from the stack exhaust could trigger an explosion (it has happened).

In port, a serious fire hazard is sometimes presented by crew members themselves. Modern tankers spend little time in port, and most tankermen try to make the most of these precious intervals. This is understandable. A freighter man can sip his beer in leisure, but the tankerman must, quite literally, "chug-a-lug" or go thirsty. Unfortunately, some individuals have perfected this art so well that they become intoxicated in short order.

To prevent these men from unwittingly lighting a cigarette in prohibited areas, and to prevent them from breaking their necks, they should be escorted to their quarters immediately upon their return to the ship.

Electrical storms. One of the first ships I worked on after getting my third mate's license was a small, multi-product tanker. She was a delightful little ship and a lot of fun to work on. Unfortunately, about a year after I left her she was struck by lightning while cleaning tanks at sea. The ensuing explosion killed and injured several men.

Lightning generates ample heat to ignite a flammable mixture. It is foolhardy (and illegal) to load, discharge, clean tanks, or transfer cargo during electrical storms.

Spontaneous combustion. Certain substances such as oily rags, oily sawdust, wet laundry, and oil-soaked rubbish are vulnerable to a process called spontaneous combustion. Slow oxidation generates heat, and over a period of days or weeks, or even months, a substance may eventually reach its ignition temperature. It then ignites *spontaneously*.

Such fires have been a problem at sea since the Phoenicians first sailed the Mediterranean thousands of years ago. More than one ship has gone to the bottom gutted by flames which started spontaneously.

Joseph Conrad dramatizes this danger in his story, "Youth," in which the bark *Judea*, carrying a cargo of coal to the Orient, catches fire and sinks in the Indian Ocean:

> You see it was to be expected, for though the coal was of a safe kind, that cargo had been so handled, so broken up with handling, that it looked more like smithy coal than anything else. Then it had been wetted—more than once. It rained all the time we were taking it back from the hulk, and now with this long passage it got heated, and there was another case of spontaneous combustion.

Cleanliness is the best weapon against spontaneous combustion. Paint lockers, laundry rooms, and other enclosed spaces must be kept as clean as possible. The chief culprits are piles of rags, rubbish, or clothing which have been impregnated with paint, grease, or vegetable oil. Such items should be laundered or disposed of promptly.

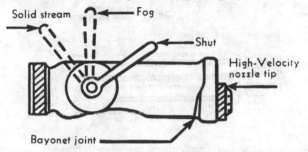

Fig. 103. All-purpose nozzle. U.S. Coast Guard.

EXTINGUISHING AGENTS AND EQUIPMENT

The following extinguishing agents are used on tankers:

Water is highly effective against *Class A* fires where a cooling effect is valuable. Sea water is generally used for this purpose.

One or more fire pumps draw water from the sea and deliver it to the fire main, a system of pipes which carries sea water to fire stations at strategic locations throughout the ship. Stop valves are fitted between stations so that sections of damaged pipe can be isolated to prevent loss of pressure.

Each fire station consists of a hydrant and fire hose (which is kept connected at all times, when practicable). In general, 2½" hose is used on weather decks, 1½" in confined spaces. Each hose is fitted with an all-purpose nozzle, which allows water to be delivered as a solid stream or in the form of high velocity fog (Fig. 103).

Low velocity fog can also be produced with special applicators (Fig. 104) which fit into the all-purpose nozzle. These break the water into a fine mist, thus presenting maximum surface area to the fire. Because of its superior cooling effect, low velocity fog is valuable as a protective "blanket" for fire fighters approaching a fire.

Fire pumps are normally located in the engine room. They are not operated except at drills and during actual emergencies. It follows that the first action after discovering a fire should be to sound the alarm, thereby alerting the engineers that pressure will soon be needed on the fire main.

Foam is particularly valuable on tankers because of its ability to form a smothering blanket over burning petroleum. Two types are used on board ship: chemical and mechanical. However, mechanical foam is far more common and has almost completely replaced the older chemical type.

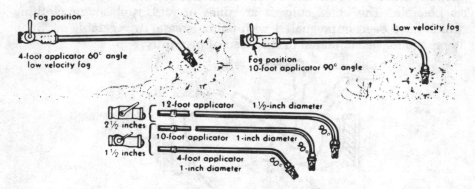

Fig. 104. Low velocity fog applicators are manufactured in various sizes and designs. U.S. Coast Guard.

Mechanical foam has three constituents: air, water, and concentrated foam liquid. The three must be mixed turbulently to produce foam with the proper characteristics. This is accomplished with specially designed nozzles which, when charged with water from the fire main, syphon foam concentrate into the line and mix it with air in the correct proportions.

Some new tankers are fitted with fixed foam systems which protect the engine room and pumproom. In addition, fixed foam monitors are often provided at main-deck fire stations (Fig. 102). Older ships are provided with portable foam nozzles fitted with pickup tubes that can be inserted into five-gallon containers of foam concentrate (Fig. 105).

The best results are obtained by directing foam onto bulkheads or other vertical surfaces adjacent to the fire and allowing it to gravitate slowly over the burning area. A stream of foam sprayed directly onto a fire should be avoided. Such action could make matters worse by agitating the fire and causing it to spread.

Foam has little cooling effect. It must therefore maintain an airtight blanket over the entire area until it has cooled sufficiently to prevent reignition. This process may take several hours.

If possible, high velocity water fog should be sprayed onto adjacent bulkheads and compartments, taking care not to break up the foam blanket. This accelerates the cooling process and prevents the fire from spreading through heat conduction.

Foam is a valuable weapon against *Class B* fires, especially spill fires on deck. In addition, foam can be used on certain *Class A* fires, although water is the preferred agent in such cases. *Foam conducts electricity* and should never be used on fires in live electrical equipment.

Regular types of foam are ineffective against water-soluble chemicals, such as alcohols and acids. A special alcohol foam must be used instead.

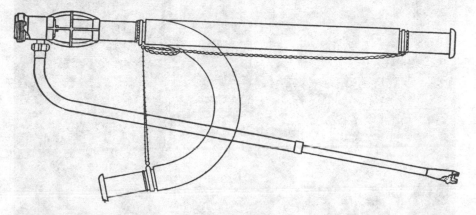

Fig. 105. Portable foam nozzle. Foam concentrate is syphoned from five-gallon containers by means of the pickup tube. Inside the nozzle, concentrate combines turbulently with water and air to produce mechanical foam. U.S. Coast Guard.

Carbon Dioxide (CO_2) is an inert gas approximately 50 percent heavier than air. It is an excellent smothering agent when used against *Class B* and *Class C* fires in confined areas.

Carbon dioxide is applied by the following methods on board ship: 1) fixed systems; 2) semiportable extinguishers; 3) portable extinguishers.

Fixed systems are most commonly used to protect the engine room, but spaces such as the pumproom, cargo tanks, and paint lockers can be fitted with their own, separate systems as well. The gas is stored in batteries of tanks in a special room (Fig. 101). Remote controls are provided in pull boxes for each space protected.

Learn where these controls are located and which spaces they serve.

Before activating a fixed CO_2 system, all ventilation to the area must be shut down and the space sealed to prevent entry of air. Fixed systems commonly contain only enough carbon dioxide for one application; they must therefore be used effectively the first time.

Carbon dioxide smothers fires effectively, but it can also smother unwary tankermen. The gas cannot be seen or smelled and gives no warning of its presence. For this reason, automatic alarms are installed on all fixed CO_2 systems. These alarms sound immediately throughout the protected spaces whenever the releasing controls are operated. A time-delay mechanism gives crew members time to leave the area before the gas is released.

Fig. 106. This sign at the engine room operating station warns crew members to evacuate when the CO_2 alarm sounds. A built-in time delay allows personnel to leave the area before gas is released. The Ansul Company.

Semiportable CO_2 extinguishers are often provided in the engine room, in addition to the usual fixed system. Tanks of carbon dioxide, bolted permanently to bulkheads, are attached to portable hoses. These hoses are stored on reels and can be run out quickly to affected areas.

Portable CO_2 extinguishers (Fig. 107) are located in bulkhead holders throughout the vessel. They are provided in spaces where *Class B* and *Class C* fires are most likely to occur, such as machine shop, radio room, galley, and pumproom.

To operate a portable CO_2 extinguisher, lift it from its holder, pull the locking pin, and squeeze the handles together. Aim the horn toward the base of the fire and apply the CO_2 in intermittent, side-to-side sweeps.

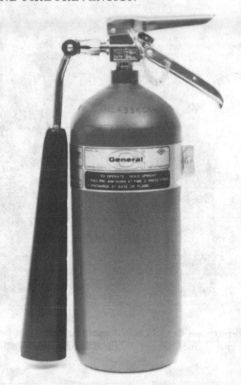

Fig. 107. Portable CO_2 extinguisher. General Fire Extinguisher Corporation.

Dry chemical extinguishing agents impede combustion by breaking up the molecular chain reaction. They are delivered with hand-held extinguishers (Fig. 108), which are located strategically throughout the vessel. Some tankers are also provided with large dry chemical units for use against spill fires on the main deck.

Dry chemical is highly effective against *Class B* and *Class C* fires, and the all-purpose type extinguisher can also be used against *Class A* fires. Dry chemical should be applied across the base of the fire in a smooth, blanketing motion. If the fire is outside, it should be approached from windward. Never spray dry chemical directly into a petroleum fire; this could agitate the fire and cause it to spread.

Steam. With the exception of the fire main, steam smothering systems are the oldest type of fire-fighting equipment found on tankers. Many older vessels are fitted with steam smothering systems, so it is important for officers to be acquainted with this equipment.

The typical steam smothering system consists of steam piping which leads from a master valve to a series of headers. A separate valve is fitted for each tank. When possible, these valves are left open; thus there is no delay in an emergency.

Fig. 108. All-purpose dry chemical extinguishers can be used on *Class A, B,* and *C* fires. General Fire Extinguisher Corporation.

Fig. 109. Halon 1211 extinguishers are effective against *Class B* and *C* fires. General Fire Extinguisher Corporation.

When fire breaks out in one of the tanks, the master valve is opened; this allows steam to flow to all of the tanks. Valves to unaffected tanks are then closed, making certain to *leave steam on in tanks adjacent to the burning compartment.* This prevents the fire from spreading through heat conduction.

After the fire has been extinguished, steam must continue to be applied until danger of reignition has passed. If turned off too soon, steam inside the tank will condense, create a vacuum, draw in air, and allow hot oil to reignite.

Every officer must know the location of the steam smothering master valve. As a rule, this valve is located at main deck level in the forward end of the engine room or inside the athwartship passageway at the forward end of the after house. Except in case of fire, this valve is kept closed. A constant steam pressure of 100 psi is maintained behind it.

Halogenated extinguishing agents, or halons, are not new to merchant ships. In the past, carbon tetrachloride served as a popular extinguishing agent. It was banned, however, because it produces toxic vapors upon contacting fire. Two new agents, Halon 1301 and Halon 1211, have recently been approved by the coast guard. Unlike carbon tetrachloride, they do not produce poisonous vapors.

The halons inhibit the chain reaction required for combustion and, to a lesser extent, tend to smother a fire with their vapors. They are most useful against *Class B* and *Class C* fires.

Halon 1301 is in some ways superior to carbon dioxide for use in fixed systems. One advantage: it is not as dangerous to personnel when breathed for short periods of time. (Like CO_2, both Halon 1301 and Halon 1211 displace oxygen upon vaporizing. Although nontoxic, they could still cause asphyxiation.)

Halon 1211 is provided in portable extinguishers (Fig. 109). Halon 1301 is provided in fixed systems protecting control rooms and similar spaces.

Inert gas. Although designed for fire prevention, inert gas systems can also be used to extinguish fires within cargo tanks. If a tank has not been ruptured (as in a collision or explosion), the addition of inert gas in sufficient quantities will lower the oxygen content below that necessary for combustion, thereby extinguishing the fire.

FIGHTING THE FIRE

Early detection and prompt, resolute action are essential to fire fighting. After a fire has been detected, the following general procedure should be followed:

1. *Sound the alarm.* A continuous sounding of general alarm and whistle will warn shipboard and shoreside personnel of danger and, equally important, will summon help.

2. *Evaluate the fire.* Above all, don't panic. Pause to think. How should this fire be fought? How can it be kept from spreading? How can sources of heat, fuel, and oxygen be eliminated? What is the greatest danger from this particular fire? How can this be blocked? A few seconds of clear, logical thought will prepare you to act decisively.

3. *Get the fire under control.* Isolate the fire by cooling surrounding bulkheads. Remove combustible material from adjacent compartments and, if possible, fill nearby cargo tanks with inert gas, CO_2, or steam. Cut off air to the fire by shutting down ventilation and by closing doors, portholes, hatches, and other openings.

4. *Extinguish the fire.* Take final steps to eradicate the fire completely: by cooling, smothering, breaking up the chain reaction, or a combination of these methods.

5. *Guard against reignition.* Make sure the affected area has cooled completely before securing fire-fighting gear. This may take several hours.

Each fire must, of course, be attacked individually. The following pages outline a general course of action for specific types of fires.

Fire in pumproom. The pumproom presents the greatest risk of cargo fires. Most pumproom fires start near the bottom of the pumproom, where they are difficult to reach. Usually, if a small fire is caught immediately it can be put out with portable foam or CO_2 extinguishers; if not, it must be fought indirectly.

One method is to hang hoses from the top of the pumproom. With all-purpose nozzles in the fog position, the fire is extinguished by a combination of cooling and smothering as water vaporizes and produces steam. Pumprooms on some vessels are fitted with fixed water fog systems which make lowering of hoses unnecessary.

Other ships are equipped with fixed CO_2, foam, or steam smothering systems. As a rule, these should be operated only after other methods have been tried. Should it become necessary to activate the fixed system, be sure the pumproom is sealed and all ventilation turned off. On some newer ships, the vent fans shut down automatically when controls to the fixed extinguishing system are operated.

After operating the fixed system, be sure to inert adjacent cargo tanks. Cool surrounding decks with water fog. If the pumproom adjoins the engine room, the bulkhead between them should also be sprayed with water.

If the fixed system is not functioning or has been depleted, it may be possible to put out the fire by sealing the pumproom as thoroughly as possible. Provided that adjacent compartments are cooled or inerted, the fire will eventually burn itself out.

After the fire has been extinguished, allow adequate cooling time before reopening. If possible, wait several hours. This precaution will avert possible reignition or explosion.

Ventilate the compartment thoroughly before allowing crew members to enter.

Fire on deck. This type of fire is usually precipitated by a spill, as from a broken hose or overflow. Therefore, the first step is to cut off the fuel supply by shutting down transfer operations. Close ullage plugs and tapewells to prevent the fire from spreading to the tanks.

Fig. 110. Foam monitor on deck. An Exxon Photo.

Foam is usually the most effective agent against fires on deck. Foam should be allowed to run gently over the fire by bouncing off bulkheads or splashing off the deck in front of the flames. Never spray foam directly onto burning oil.

Dry chemical, if available in sufficient quantities, is also effective against spill fires. It should be applied from upwind if possible (at sea this can be accomplished by changing the ship's course as necessary).

Fire in cargo tank. A quantity of oil which has been on fire a short time is hot on the surface but relatively cool underneath. For example, fuel oil which has burned 10 to 12 minutes heats to its ignition

Fig. 111. This semiportable CO_2 system employs a hose reel and two fixed cylinders. The hose is reeled out, then charged with CO_2 by opening the cylinder valves. The gas is directed at the fire by operating the control lever on the discharge horn. The Ansul Company.

temperature to a depth of only one inch. If extinguished quickly, it requires relatively little time to cool to a safe temperature.

A fire in an unruptured cargo tank should be fought in the following sequence.

1. Shut off the air supply by closing tank tops, ullage plugs, tank cleaning openings, tapewells, and PV valves.

2. Activate fixed CO_2, inert gas, or steam smothering system. After opening the master valve, close valves to unaffected tanks. Make sure, however, that tanks adjacent to the fire are protected.

3. Cool nearby decks, bulkheads, and equipment with high velocity water fog.

4. If the air supply cannot be cut off, direct foam through the tank top and allow it to spread over the fire. Unfortunately, this method is only effective in a full or nearly full tank. In an empty tank, it is necessary for the foam to coat every exposed surface where oil has been deposited, i.e., deck, keel, beams, frames, bulkheads, etc. This is virtually impossible. In such a case, high velocity water fog should be used.

When a tank has been ruptured (as by explosion or collision), the fixed system is often useless. Foam or water fog should be used. Water should be applied with caution. Be particularly careful not to agitate the surface of burning oil. If foam and water are used simultaneously, be careful not to break up, dilute, or wash away the foam blanket with the water.

Fire in engine room. Most engine room fires can be extinguished with portable or semiportable extinguishers (Fig. 111). Larger fires should be fought with fixed or portable foam systems, plus water fog from the fire main.

Fire fighters entering the burning area must wear a lifeline plus breathing apparatus for protection against asphyxiation and smoke inhalation.

Use the fixed CO_2 system as a last resort only. These systems often provide only one application; it must not be wasted. Before activating the fixed system, clear the area of personnel; close doors, hatches, and vents; secure boiler fires and vent fans. Controls for the CO_2 system and engine room ventilation are located outside the engine room. Learn the location of these controls before you need them; don't be caught unprepared in an emergency.

While the CO_2 is being released, spray water fog on outside decks and bulkheads. Remove combustible material, which could ignite through heat conduction, from neighboring areas. After the fire has been extinguished, allow adequate time for the compartment to cool before reopening.

Fig. 112. Close-up of cylinder valves and attachments used with the semiportable CO_2 system. The Ansul Company.

Remember: If the fire flares up again, there may be inadequate CO_2 to put it out a second time.

Fire on water adjacent to ship. This type of fire often occurs after a collision. Foam is the most effective weapon. Bounce foam off the ship's hull so that it flows gently over the fire. If the fire is too far from the hull for this method to work, deliver foam to a spot near the burning area. Pool it so that it flows easily over the fire; do not apply directly.

Fig. 113. Halon 1211 and CO_2 extinguishers are effective against small electrical fires and leave no residue to foul contacts. General Fire Extinguisher Corporation.

If no foam is available, solid streams of water may be sprayed between ship and fire. When conditions permit, this tactic will induce a surface current and move the fire clear of the ship.

Fire in live electrical equipment. If possible, de-energize the equipment. Should you have the slightest doubt, however, assume the equipment is "hot" and act accordingly.

Never spray water on live electrical equipment. Salt water is an excellent conductor; fire fighters using it run the risk of being electrocuted. Foam is equally dangerous. (In theory, low velocity water fog does not conduct electricity and can be used on electrical fires. This is at best a risky proposition.)

Carbon dioxide and the halons are the preferred agents against electrical fires, since they leave no residue (Fig. 113). Dry chemical

Fig. 114. Breathing apparatus must be worn when fighting fires in enclosed spaces. ATO, Inc.

extinguishers can also be used, but they deposit a fine powder which may foul electrical contacts.

Fire in living spaces. This generally involves a *Class A* fire, making water the preferred extinguishing agent. Keep all doors to the compartment closed until equipment is assembled and ready for use. Cool outside bulkheads and doors with water. When ready to enter, fire fighters should use low velocity fog as a forward shield against heat and smoke. All crew members entering the compartment must wear lifelines and breathing apparatus (Fig. 114).

Fire on dock. When a fire occurs on the dock or adjacent area, your first concern as officer in charge should be the safety of your ship. Take immediate steps to move her. Shut down the cargo, disconnect hoses and loading arms, single up lines, and have the engineers put steam on the engines. Call tugs if necessary.

If a strong tide is running and no obstructions lie downstream, simply throw off mooring lines and allow the vessel to drift to safety. When well clear, drop the anchor.

PREVENTION VERSUS CURE

The threat of fire, whether recognized or not, is always present on a tanker. Some crew members may go about their jobs in blissful ignorance, unmindful of the destructive force lurking beneath their feet, but you, as an officer, cannot afford to become complacent.

A tanker fire is a terrifying thing, difficult and dangerous to put out. Tankermen must always be prepared for the worst. But hopefully, if you and your shipmates remain alert and careful, the worst will never happen.

Chapter 10

PREVENTING POLLUTION: THE TANKERMAN'S ROLE

Several years ago I decided to take a short break from tankers and shipped out as third mate on a passenger ship. During my seven months on board, she made three passages through the Strait of Magellan at the southern edge of South America.

Fig. 115. Bow-on view of a 326,000-tonner. The consequences of a collision involving such a ship could be disastrous. Improved navigation and collision avoidance systems, rigidly enforced sea lanes, and shore-based radar control may help to prevent such an occurrence. Gulf Oil Corporation.

Each was a memorable experience.

Like a delicate ribbon of blue silk, the waterway turned and weaved through a magnificent panorama of fjords, glaciers, and snowcapped mountains. The ship, a man-made object, seemed out of place as it glided through this virtually unblemished place.

But even the most remote spots are vulnerable to man's technology, and the Strait of Magellan is no exception. In August of 1974, about a year after my final trip on the passenger ship, I was shocked to hear that a supertanker had run aground on the rocky shores of Magellan Strait. She was the *Metula*, a 206,000-d.w.t. VLCC.

Not only was the ship badly damaged, but over 50,000 tons of crude oil flooded from her torn hull onto adjacent water and shoreline. At this writing, the oil remains on the shore and continues to seep into surrounding waters. Scientists have predicted that it will continue as a source of pollution for years to come.

In an area of abundant and diverse wildlife such as the Strait of Magellan, the long-term effect could be devastating.

WHAT CAUSES POLLUTION?

Spills from tanker groundings, collisions, and similar accidents are among the most obvious sources of oil pollution.

For example, when the fully laden Liberian tanker *Torrey Canyon* (120,000 d.w.t.) strayed off course and broke up on the rocks near the Scilly Isles in 1967, thousands of barrels of crude oil drifted ashore. Citizens of Britain and France reacted angrily to the fouling of their beaches and the killing of fish and sea birds.

In December of 1976, citizens of the United States were similarly outraged when another Liberian tanker, the *Argo Merchant*, broke up on a shoal off Nantucket Island. Her full cargo, 180,000 barrels of heavy industrial fuel, poured into the sea, creating the worst spill in the history of the U.S. Atlantic coast.

Such spectacular accidents are a serious source of pollution, but they account for only about 10 percent of the oil dumped into the world's oceans each year. In fact, a large percentage of oil discharges come from sources other than tankers. Shore terminals, naval vessels, and freighters are a few of the chief offenders on a very long list.

However, these other sources of pollution are beyond our control as tankermen; we have to concentrate on preventing discharges of oil from *tankers*.

The most important sources of tanker pollution, in order of magnitude, are as follows: 1) routine discharges during ballasting and tank cleaning; 2) collisions and groundings; 3) accidental spills while loading and discharging.

The first—routine discharges—accounts for about four times as much oil pollution as the other two combined. Routine discharges therefore pose the most insidious threat to marine ecology.

It is also interesting to note that lighter refined products, such gasoline and jet fuel, are more deadly to sea life than heavy crude fuel oils. The latter, although they float thick, black, and greasy surface, do not dissolve quickly and therefore are not readily ingested by fish and water mammals. Refined products, on the other hand, contain poisonous elements which dissolve in water and become invisible while remaining highly poisonous to fish and other sea life.

Fig. 116. This 70,000-d.w.t. Liberian tanker, the *Wafra*, ran onto a reef after suffering engine failure near Cape Agulhas, South Africa, in 1971. Nearly half her 63,000-ton cargo of crude spilled into the sea. The ship was a total loss. U.S. Salvage Association.

In this chapter we will explore some of the ways in which oil pollution can be prevented. Improvements continue to be made in tanker design and equipment, but improved technology is not enough to solve the problem. Human beings control the machines, and the ultimate responsibility rests on their shoulders.

Tankermen, especially officers, share an important part of this responsibility.

MINIMIZING ROUTINE DISCHARGES

Just a few years ago, it was a common practice to pump tank ashings and dirty ballast overboard at sea. As a result huge quantities oil were dumped into the oceans of the world.

was normal, for example, while cleaning tanks en route to the rd, to pour a steady stream of "muck" into the sea for days on end, leaving a trail of oil hundreds of miles long. I've seen it; in fact, I've pumped my own share of oil into the ocean in just that manner. At the time, we took this practice for granted as perfectly normal and legal (which it was). But those days are over.

The *International Convention for the Prevention of Pollution from Ships, 1973*, drawn up by the maritime nations of the world, places strict limits on the amount of oil discharged on the high seas. Slops are now retained on board for eventual discharge to shore facilities or, in the case of crude carriers, are commingled with the next cargo. Only clean ballast is discharged along coastlines.

As we discussed in Chapter 7, tankers must ballast their tanks when empty in order to remain seaworthy. Unfortunately, when sea water is pumped into cargo tanks as ballast it inevitably washes residual oil from tank surfaces and, when discharged to sea, carries part of the oil with it. This is *dirty ballast*.

Despite the stringent requirements dictated by the 1973 Convention, ships must still ballast their tanks. And of course tanks still have to be cleaned periodically. The problem is to dispose of slops and dirty ballast without pumping them overboard.

On the following pages we will explore some of the ways in which this problem is solved.

Segregated ballast tanks. One obvious solution to the problem of dirty ballast is not to create any.

The 1973 Convention requires all new tankers of 70,000 d.w.t. and over to be fitted with separate clean ballast tanks incorporating an independent pump and piping system. Ballast is thus kept free of oil and can be pumped into and out of the tanks at will with no risk of pollution.

Generally speaking, at least one pair of wing tanks is tied into the clean ballast system (cargo piping, if installed, must be blanked off). Forepeak and afterpeak tanks are also used, and a few vessels are fitted with double bottom tanks for this purpose.

It is interesting to note that, at this writing, the Department of Transportation is drawing up regulations which, if adopted, will require all new tankers of more than 20,000 d.w.t. to be fitted with double bottom tanks for clean ballast. This requirement will apply to American tankers and also to foreign vessels calling at American ports.

Load-on-top system (LOT). In the early 1960s Shell International Petroleum voluntarily implemented a new system of ballast handling on its crude carriers: the load-on-top system, or LOT. Other major oil companies followed Shell's example, and today load-on-top is a standard practice on tankers.

Authorities estimate that use of load-on-top has reduced tanker discharges by over three million tons per year. This figure represents a

'Load on top' system of controlling pollution at sea

After discharging cargo, a tanker requires quantities of sea-water in some of its tanks to serve as ballast. When the water is loaded it mixes with oil residues in the tanks and becomes 'dirty'. During the voyage this dirty ballast water has to be replaced by clean ballast which can be pumped back to the sea without risk of pollution when the tanker reaches the loading port. Some empty tanks must therefore be cleaned at sea to ensure that the sea-water pumped into them as ballast remains clean and free of oil.

1 During the voyage tanks to be filled with clean ballast water are washed and the oily washings are collected into one slop tank.

The oil in the neighbouring 'dirty ballast' tanks floats to the top.

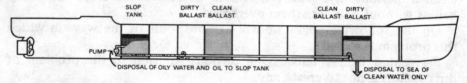

2 The now clean tanks are filled with ballast water which will remain clean and suitable for discharge at the loading port.

In the 'dirty ballast' tanks, the clean water under the oil is discharged to the sea and the oily layer on top is transferred to the slop tank.

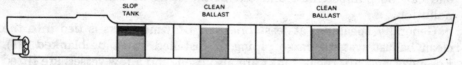

3 In the slop tank, the dirty washings and the oil from the dirty ballast settle into a layer of oil floating on clean sea-water.

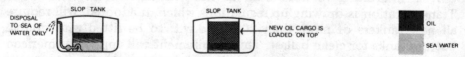

4 This clean water under the oil is carefully pumped back into the sea and the oily waste left on board. The next cargo is loaded on top of the remaining oil and all of it is discharged when the tanker berths at the refinery.

Fig. 117. How load-on-top works. Shell International Petroleum.

180

substantial reduction in worldwide pollution, plus a savings in recovered oil to companies.

Figure 117 shows how the load-on-top system works.

At the discharging port the ship pumps water ballast into selected empty cargo tanks in the usual manner. On the voyage to the loading port, other tanks are washed in preparation for clean ballast. (Each branch line is flushed first by pumping a few barrels of sea water into tanks which are to be cleaned.)

Tank cleaning slops are pumped into the aftermost center tank and retained on board. The newly cleaned tanks are then filled with ballast which, if the tanks have been washed properly, should be clean enough to pump overboard.

In the meantime the initial dirty ballast has had time to settle out; that is, free-oil in the ballast has had time to float to the surface. Most of the clean bottom water can therefore be pumped overboard (to within perhaps five feet of the bottom). The remaining water and oil are then stripped to the slop tank.

The slop tank is allowed to settle in the same manner before pumping out the clean bottom water. It is important to drain off as much of this water as possible, since any remaining in the slop tank must be commingled with the next cargo.

Pumping this water overboard is a delicate task; it should be done slowly and carefully. It is difficult to determine the precise position of the interface between clean water and floating oil, so there is always a risk of pumping some oil overboard. This should be guarded against.

On some tankers, pumproom oil-in-water detectors have been used successfully to combat this problem. In addition, it is likely that accurate monitoring equipment will soon be developed for locating the oil interface in slop tanks.

After following the procedures just described, a tanker is, for all practical purposes, in clean ballast. Before any of this ballast is pumped overboard, however, it may be necessary to flush the pumps and bottom piping into the slop tank as discussed in Chapter 8. This is done before draining the bottom water from the slop tank, so that additional water introduced while flushing can also be settled out and discharged.

Upon arrival at the loading port, a small amount of emulsified oil and water will remain in the slop tank. The new cargo can be "loaded on top" and commingled with this mixture with no adverse effect.

Discharging slops and dirty ballast to shore facilities. The load-on-top technique works well on crude carriers making long ballast passages, but it cannot be used by all tankers. For example, on ships carrying refined products, loading on top would produce serious contamination in most cargoes.

Vessels making short hauls along the coast are also unable to use load-on-top, for two reasons:

1. Slops and ballast must have sufficient time to settle before draining off bottom water. A short voyage does not permit adequate settling.

2. It is illegal to pump *any* oil overboard within the *prohibited zone* (that is, within 50 miles of the coast—farther in some areas). The load-on-top system, no matter how effective, involves the release of some oil.

Product carriers and tankers making short hauls along the coast must therefore deal with slops and dirty ballast in another manner. One obvious answer is to pump slops ashore at the loading terminal, where they can be processed in shore separators. Because product carriers load nearly all of their cargoes at refineries, where facilities for handling slops and dirty ballast are available, this has become the logical solution to their dirty ballast problem.

Tankers entering dry dock for repairs also face a problem of slop disposal. Luckily, nearly all major repair yards in the world are now provided with facilities capable of handling a substantial volume of dirty ballast and slops.

Vessels cleaning tanks for the shipyard therefore use a modified form of the load-on-top system. On the sea passage to the yard, tanks are cleaned and ballast transferred in the usual manner. Upon arrival, instead of "loading on top" as would normally occur at a loading terminal, slops are stripped ashore.

Waterless (crude oil) washing of tanks greatly reduces the amount of slop water created and thus lessens the problem of slop disposal.

The crude washing technique has proven effective and is gaining popularity on crude carriers. Crude oil, drawn from the ship's cargo, is sprayed onto tank surfaces with the regular, fixed machines. If necessary, the crude oil wash is followed by a water rinse.

See Chapter 8 for a further discussion of the crude washing technique.

COLLISIONS AND GROUNDINGS

The waterways of the world are more crowded than ever before; ships of all types, not just tankers, run greater risk of collision. European sailors have battled this problem for years—a trip through the English Channel, North Sea, or Mediterranean is a nerve-wracking experience for even the sharpest watch officer. But ships are bigger than they used to be and the consequences of a collision, especially one involving a tanker, are much greater. The old hit-and-miss methods of dodging other ships are no longer acceptable.

Maritime nations have recently taken steps to control ship movements more precisely. Most notable has been the introduction of traffic lanes in congested waterways such as the English Channel, the Strait of Malacca, and the Cape of Good Hope (and on approaches to major harbors such as New York).

Radar monitoring of ship movements has also been used effectively in harbors and in such areas as the Strait of Dover (through which a large portion of Europe's tanker traffic must pass).

Fig. 118. Automated bridge of a modern tanker. Improved navigation equipment helps to minimize chances of collision and grounding. Kockums Automation AB.

Improvements have been made in shipboard navigation equipment, which now includes computer assisted collision avoidance systems. Aids to navigation are also being improved. An example is *RACON*, an electronic system which provides positive radar identification of geographic points.

With the advent of VLCCs, groundings have become a more serious risk than in previous years. Many nautical charts in use today were made for ships drawing about 30 feet; some are based on surveys from the 19th century.

Today hundreds of ships drawing 60, 70, 80 feet and over are plying "shallow" waters, previously deep enough for any ship, with no real

Fig. 119. Outbound from the Persian Gulf, British officers navigate a
VLCC down the east coast of Africa. Destination: Western Europe via
the Cape of Good Hope. Photo by The British Petroleum Co. Ltd.

assurance that they won't strike bottom. In fact, a few have struck
bottom, most notably in the Strait of Malacca near Singapore, where
the bottom is granite.

It is hoped that improved surveys and more precise depthfinding
equipment will eventually solve these problems. In addition,
government and industry researchers are working on long range sonar
systems which will probe the waters ahead of deep-draft vessels.

Another solution is to keep VLCCs out of shallow water. Because
these vessels draw too much water to enter major harbors anyway, they
often call at offshore terminals where they load and discharge through
submerged pipelines.

Over a hundred of these terminals now use single-point moorings, or SPMs (Fig. 120). An underwater pipeline carries cargo along the ocean floor to the shore terminal, often miles away. Deep-draft tankers thus avoid the uncomfortable task of feeling their way into shallow harbors.

The job of piloting a VLCC, whether in a harbor or along the coast, is a tricky one. A variety of sophisticated equipment has been developed to make the job easier—bow and stern thrusters, doppler speed indicators, etc. However, different ships use different equipment and this sometimes confuses pilots. For this reason, it is extremely important for the master and other officers to assist pilots in every way possible and to advise them about the ship's maneuvering characteristics.

Some companies use a form (Fig. 121) to make sure important information is exchanged between pilot and ship's master.

PREVENTING SPILLS

Accidental spills while loading and discharging account for only a small portion of total pollution. They are nevertheless a constant worry—perhaps the greatest worry of all—for tankermen.

If you have a spill, even a small one, the consequences to you personally may be devastating, involving huge fines and possible loss of your license. Prevention of such spills is therefore vital, not only for the protection of harbors and coastlines, but of your own well-being.

Some common sources of spills are described in the following paragraphs.

Hoses and loading arms. These form at best a delicate bond, easily broken, between ship's riser and shore pipeline.

Flexible hoses with flanged couplings are connected by inserting a fiber gasket (use once only) between flanges, which are secured with no less than four bolts, one in every other hole. This is an important operation and must be done carefully. In ports where loading arms take the place of hoses, a special hydraulic clamp is sometimes used in lieu of the conventional hookup with bolts. Quick connect/disconnect hoses are also used on some ships.

Whichever method is used, the connection should be made with deliberate attention and care.

Flexible hoses should be supported by belt slings, saddles, or bridles, *not a single rope sling* (Fig. 122). These are hung from hose booms provided in the manifold area. They should be placed approximately every ten feet along the length of the hose. Topping lifts and runners supporting hoses should be *made fast to cleats*, never left on capstans or gypsy heads.

Loading arms are in some ways superior to hoses, but they can tolerate little fore-and-aft movement. A strong surge forward or aft can snap loading arms like so many matchsticks. The result is not just a

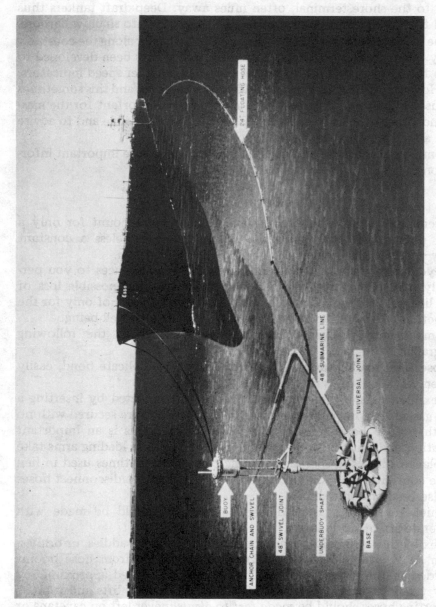

Fig. 120. Schematic diagram of a single-point mooring at Marsa el Brega, Libya. An Exxon Photo.

spill, but a deluge. The way to prevent this problem is to tend mooring lines carefully and to keep risers and loading arms aligned as closely as possible.

Small spills frequently occur when hoses and loading arms are drained before disconnecting. Hoses are normally drained into ship's tanks, blown clear with compressed air, sucked out with shore pumps, or simply drained into drip pans. Whichever method is used, make sure it is done carefully. After disconnecting, have crew members attach blank flanges to hoses, loading arms, and manifold connections (Fig. 124).

A common mistake occurs when crew members forget to bleed air into the line as hoses are being sucked out by shore pumps. This creates a vacuum which holds oil in the hose. As a result, oil sometimes floods out on deck when the hose connection is broken.

In the event that some oil does leak out for any reason, never allow the sailors to drain it overboard by pulling scupper plugs. It is amazing how many veteran seamen still try to get away with this. It may save them a messy cleanup job, but it won't get you anywhere but in trouble.

Communication. Language differences can cause plenty of trouble in foreign countries. Be sure to reach a clear understanding with the shore as to which language will be used, and make sure everyone involved understands signals for starting and stopping cargo.

Communication is sometimes a source of difficulty at offshore terminals where radios are used. Be sure to know which frequency the shore is using. In addition, specify an emergency shutdown signal (usually a long blast of the ship's whistle) in case the radio malfunctions.

Equipment failure. Many spills have been caused by jammed valves and broken ullage tapes. These spills are difficult to prevent, since the equipment may seem to be working fine. For example, a gate valve may "feel" closed after turning down 25 turns when in reality it has jammed with five turns to go.

Such spills can, however, be minimized and contained by alert watch standing. Be on guard for malfunctions and never assume your equipment is flawless; it isn't.

Sea valves. Improperly set sea valves have been the source of some disastrous spills. Following is an example of how this could happen.

A tanker on the final leg of her ballast passage approaches the loading port. Sea valves are opened and ballast is discharged to sea. For one reason or another, the pumpman forgets to close the sea valves afterwards. The ship arrives at the dock and the officers complete the preloading checkoff—neglecting, however, to check the sea valves.

Loading commences. It is nighttime and a strong tide is running. Hundreds of barrels of oil flow silently into the harbor via the open sea

Before proceeding on pilotage, please give the following information to the vessel Master:

1. What is your intended plan of navigation and approach to the berth?

2. How many tugs will be used?

3. When and where will tugs make fast?

4. Will ship's lines be used for tugs?

5. What are the tide and current conditions along the route?

6. What is the force and direction of wind expected along the route?

7. What visibility conditions do you anticipate?

8. Available anchorage en route?

During pilotage, develop a specific berthing plan with the Master. Pay particular attention to angle and velocity of approach to the jetty, line running sequence, and the tug/mooring boat control system. Develop this plan in sufficient time for it to be explained to the ship's officers. If necessary, develop an alternative plan to use if things should go wrong.

Take your time. Slow down, if necessary, to ensure that all parties agree to proposed action.

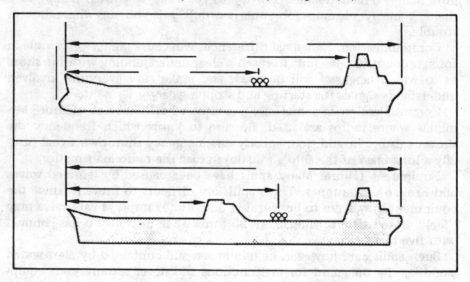

Prepared by _____ . Master

Read and understood _____ . Pilot

Fig. 121. Vessel/Pilot Information Exchange form. Atlantic Richfield Company.

valves. Unnoticed by crew members, it drifts into the darkness with the tide.

To avoid this type of spill, always check sea valves carefully before loading starts. In fact, it is wise for two officers to do so independently. *This inspection is essential; don't neglect it.* It is also important to make regular checks of the water around your vessel during cargo watches, day and night. If you see anything that looks like oil, shut down until you find out where it's coming from.

Fig. 122. Flexible hoses should be supported by belt slings, saddles, or bridles. Chevron Shipping Company.

WHAT TO DO IF YOU HAVE A SPILL

Quick and intelligent action can minimize the effects of a spill. Should a spill occur while you are in charge, resulting in the leaking of oil to harbor waters, take the following steps immediately:

1. Shut down and close valves from which oil is escaping.
2. Call the master and chief mate and tell them what has happened.
3. Alert the engine room and have them pressurize the fire main, if necessary. Have crew members break out fire-fighting gear.
4. Notify the terminal.
5. In an American port, call the coast guard by radio or telephone and report the spill. Give your name and title, vessel name, company

Fig. 123. Loading arms can tolerate little fore-and-aft movement. Mooring lines must be tended carefully to maintain alignment with risers and to prevent surges forward or aft. A Shell Photo.

Fig. 124. Cargo hoses must be blanked off after disconnecting. An Exxon Photo.

Fig. 125. Proper communication between ship and terminal is essential. Chevron
Shipping Company.

name, location of spill, and approximate quantity of oil involved. The
law requires you to make this report as soon as possible after discovering a spill. The fine for noncompliance is $10,000.

LAWS GOVERNING POLLUTION CONTROL

There are numerous Federal, state, and local laws relating to pollution, all of which must be obeyed by tankermen. Most notable are the
Oil Pollution Act of 1961 and the Federal Water Pollution Control Act.
Essentially, these laws prohibit the discharge of oil in harbors and
coastal regions of the United States and provide stiff penalties for
violators.

Prohibited zones extend 50 miles from the coast in most areas and to
greater distances along special shorelines. Within these zones *no oil
whatsoever* may be discharged. Clean ballast may be discharged only if
it would not leave a sheen on the water in calm weather.

The U.S. Coast Guard has written a set of Pollution Prevention Regulations, based on Federal laws. They are included in *CG-123, Rules and
Regulations for Tank Vessels* (carried on all American tankers).

1973 CONVENTION

In the Fall of 1973, representatives of the maritime nations met in
London and drafted the *International Convention for the Prevention of
Pollution from Ships, 1973.*

The Convention prohibits the discharge of oil and oily mixtures within 50 miles from nearest land. Discharges are also prohibited within certain "special areas" (Mediterranean, Baltic, Black, and Red Seas, and the Persian Gulf). Ballast water discharged in the prohibited zones may contain no more than 15 parts per million of oil—a miniscule amount.

Unlike regulations passed by individual countries, the 1973 Convention covers the whole world. It is administered by the Inter-Governmental Maritime Consultative Organization (IMCO), an agency of the United Nations.

Besides establishing prohibited zones, the Convention limits the amount of oil discharged outside these zones (that is, on the high seas). The total oil discharged, per voyage, may not exceed 1/15,000 of a tanker's deadweight tonnage (1/30,000 on new tankers). The instantaneous flow rate may not exceed 60 liters per mile. This is a very small quantity of oil considering what tankers used to dump into the ocean. Future conventions will, in all likelihood, completely prohibit the discharge of oil on the high seas.

In addition, the 1973 Convention limits the size of tanks on new ships and requires all new tankers of 70,000 d.w.t. and over to be fitted with segregated ballast tanks.

THE OIL RECORD BOOK

Figure 126 shows a sample page from the *Oil Record Book*, which is distributed to American ships by the U.S. Coast Guard. Ships of other nations use a similar form.

Officers are required to use the *Oil Record Book* to keep a record of all cargo, ballast, and tank cleaning activities. This must include the time, date, ship's position, and other relevant details for each of the following operations:

1. Loading of oil cargo.
2. Transfer of oil cargo during voyage.
3. Discharge of oil cargo.
4. Ballasting of cargo tanks.
5. Cleaning of cargo tanks.
6. Discharge of dirty ballast.
7. Discharge of water from slop tanks.
8. Disposal of residues.
9. Spills or other accidental discharges of oil.

The chief mate may choose to fill in these items himself or he may delegate the task to another officer. No matter who is chosen to do the job, it is important to keep the entries up-to-date. The coast guard makes frequent spot checks on tankers in American ports, and the *Oil Record Book* is one of the first things they scrutinize.

NAME OF VESSEL | OFFICIAL NO. | TOTAL CARGO CARRYING CAPACITY OF SHIP IN CUBIC METRES | PART I

A. LOADING OF OIL CARGO

1. DATE AND PLACE OF LOADING
2. TYPES OF OIL LOADED
3. IDENTITY OF TANK(S) LOADED

B. TRANSFER OF OIL CARGO DURING VOYAGE

4. DATE OF TRANSFER
5. IDENTITY OF TANK(S) — i FROM — ii TO
6. WAS (WERE) TANK(S) IN 5(i) EMPTIED

C. DISCHARGE OF OIL CARGO

7. DATE AND PLACE OF DISCHARGE
8. IDENTITY OF TANK(S) DISCHARGED
9. WAS (WERE) TANK(S) EMPTIED

D. BALLASTING OF CARGO TANKS

10. IDENTITY OF TANK(S) BALLASTED
11. DATE AND POSITION OF SHIP AT START OF BALLASTING

E. CLEANING OF CARGO TANKS

12. IDENTITY OF TANK(S) CLEANED
13. DATE AND DURATION OF CLEANING
14. METHODS OF CLEANING *

REMARKS

SIGNATURE OF OFFICER OR OFFICER IN CHARGE OF OPERATION CONCERNED

SIGNATURE OF MASTER

* Hand hosing, machine washing or chemical cleaning, where chemically cleaned, the chemical concerned and the amount used should be stated.

Fig. 126. Sample page from the *Oil Record Book* (Part 1). U.S. Coast Guard.

KEEP IT IN THE TANKS

Thor Heyerdahl, the Norwegian explorer, made an epic crossing of the North Atlantic on his raft, *Ra*, in 1969. His 57-day voyage started in Morocco and ended in Barbados in the Caribbean.

Heyerdahl made the following statement about his passage:

". . . at least a continuous stretch of 1,400 miles of the open Atlantic is polluted by floating lumps of solidified, asphalt-like oil."

Many people still think the seas, in their vastness, will remain forever immune to danger from man's influence. This is a naive belief. The seas are vast but not infinite; they can absorb just so much oil.

Spilled oil is the potential enemy of all living creatures, human beings included. It destroys or limits the growth of marine life, ruins wildlife nesting areas along shores, spoils beaches and recreation areas, kills birds, contaminates drinking water, causes fire hazards, and releases noxious vapors.

In plain words, the most important duty of every tankerman is to keep the oil where it belongs—in the tanks.

BIBLIOGRAPHY

Baptist, C., *Tanker Handbook for Deck Officers*, 1975.

CG-174, A Manual for the Safe Handling of Inflammable and Combustible Liquids and Other Hazardous Products, U.S. Coast Guard, 1975.

CG-329, Fire Fighting Manual for Tank Vessels, U.S. Coast Guard, 1974.

"Crude Tanker Pollution Abatement," Exxon Position Paper, Exxon Corporation, April, 1976.

"Crude Washing of Tankers," Salen & Wicander AB.

Franklin, Ted, "Inert Gas Systems for Tankers: What They Are, How They Work," *Marine Engineering/Log*, January, 1975.

Gardner, A. Ward, and Page, R.C., *Petroleum Tankship Safety*, 1971.

Jimenez, Richard, "The Evolution of the Load Line," *Surveyor*, May, 1976.

King, G.A.B., *Tanker Practice*, 1971.

"LNG/LPG Update," *Marine Engineering/Log*, September, 1976.

Mostert, Noel, *Supership*, 1975.

Tanker Cleaning Manual, Gamlen Chemical Company.

"VLCCs," Exxon Background Series, Exxon Corporation, November, 1975.

INDEX